The New Generation of
MANGA ARTISTS
Vol. 7 Special edition
NOUVEIS LOGIC

THE NEW GENERATAION OF MANGA ARTISTS
VOL. 7: Special edition, NOUVEIS LOGIC

Copyright © 2005 Kazuaki Kawashima
Copyright © 2005 Hiroyuki Karashima
Copyright © 2005 Graphic-sha Publishing Co., Ltd.

This book was first designed and published in Japan in 2005 by Graphic-sha Publishing Co., Ltd.
This English edition was published in 2005 by Graphic-sha Publishing Co., Ltd.,
Sansou Kudan Bldg., 4th Floor, 1-14-17 Kudan-kita, Chiyoda-ku, Tokyo 102-0073, Japan.

Special thanks to: A.W.S. (Anime World Star)

Original cover design and text page layout:	Shinichi Ishioka
English translation management:	Língua fránca, Inc. (an3y-skmt@asahi-net.or.jp)
Planning editor:	Kuniyoshi Masujima (Graphic-sha Publishing Co., Ltd.)
Publishing coordinator:	Michiko Yasu (Graphic-sha Publishing Co., Ltd.)
Project management:	Kumiko Sakamoto (Graphic-sha Publishing Co., Ltd.)

First printing: May 2005

ISBN: 4-7661-1469-8
Printed and bound in China by Everbest Printing Co., Ltd.

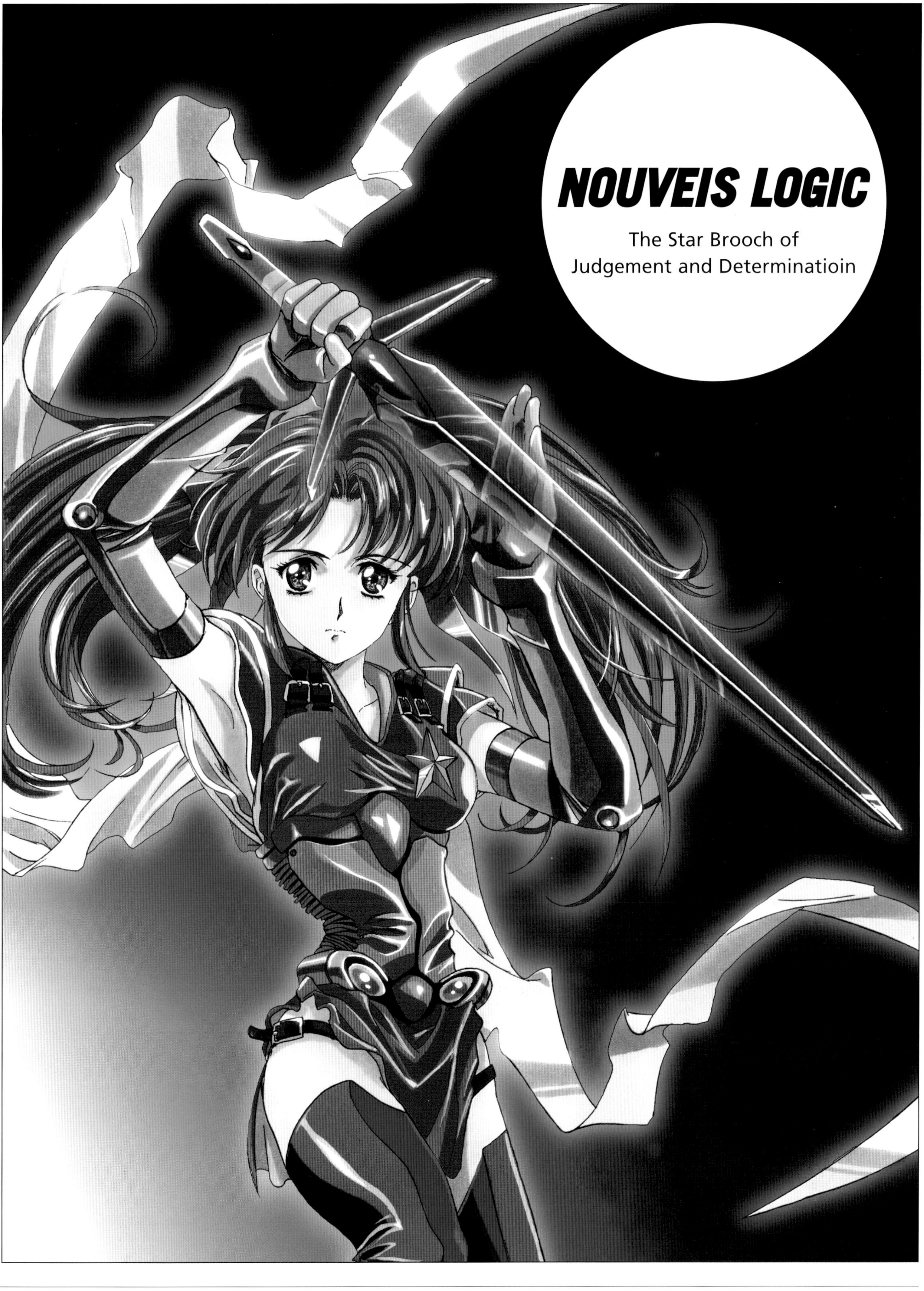
NOUVEIS LOGIC
The Star Brooch of
Judgement and Determinatioin

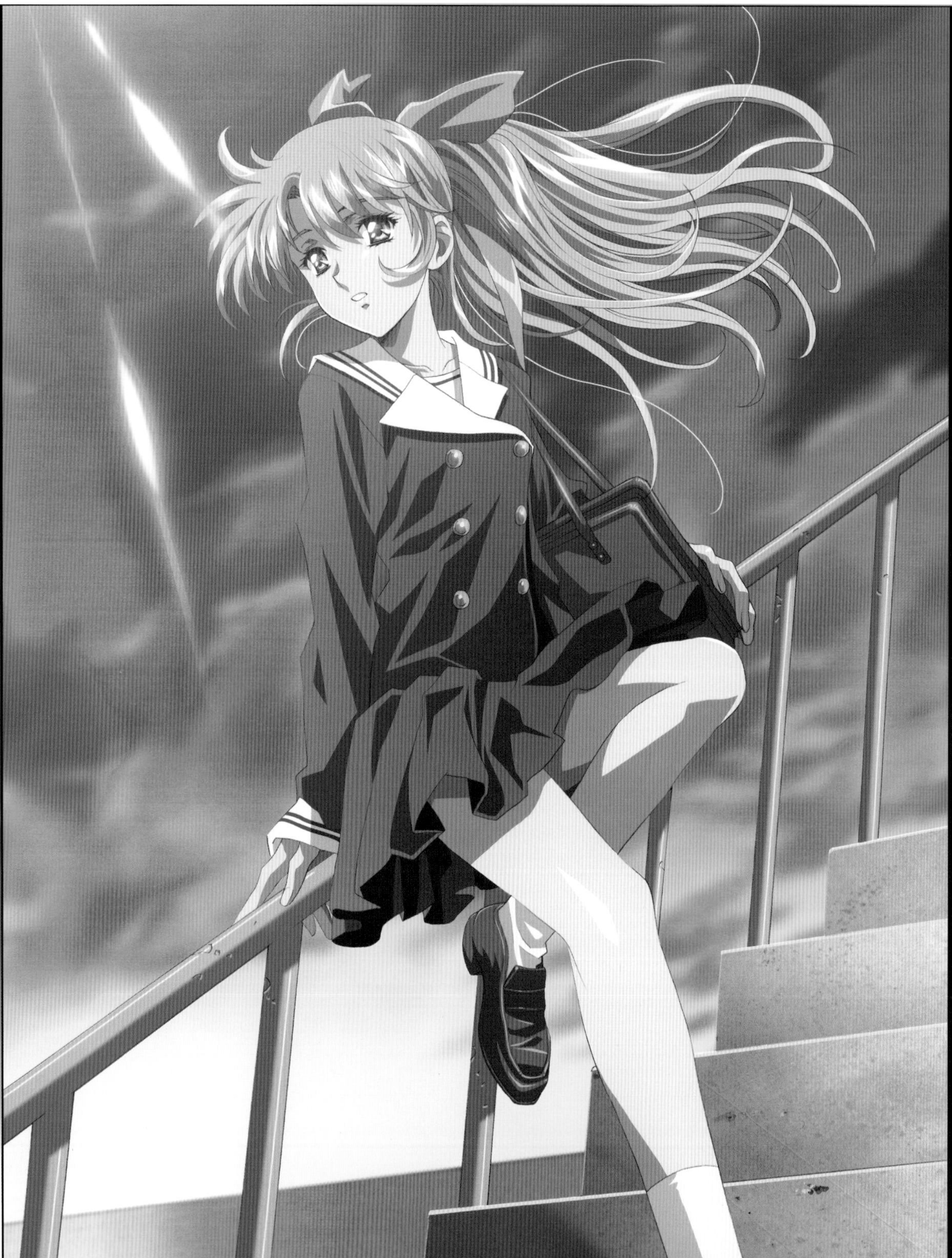

From some time ago, the young girl had begun her wait to encounter once again the boy who played the ocarina flute, who she had met on this very spot. She waited eagerly, while listening to the quiet waves beating against the twilight-bathed shore.

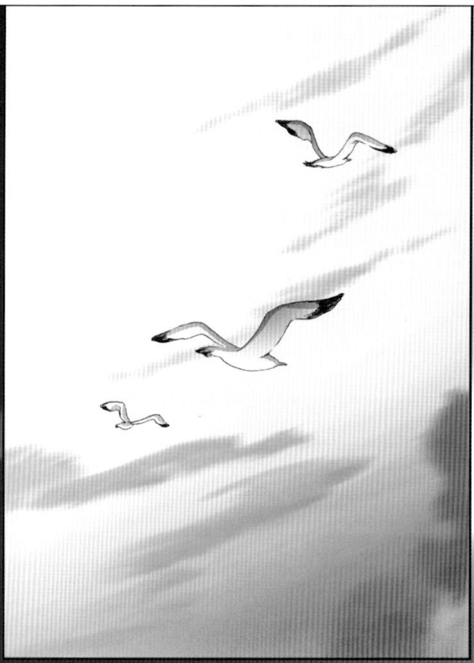

This encounter did not happen long ago at some time lost to memory, but rather at a time countable in days, since not even a month had passed. Nonetheless, perhaps the passage of time felt so monumentally long, because the meeting had suddenly become precious to her.

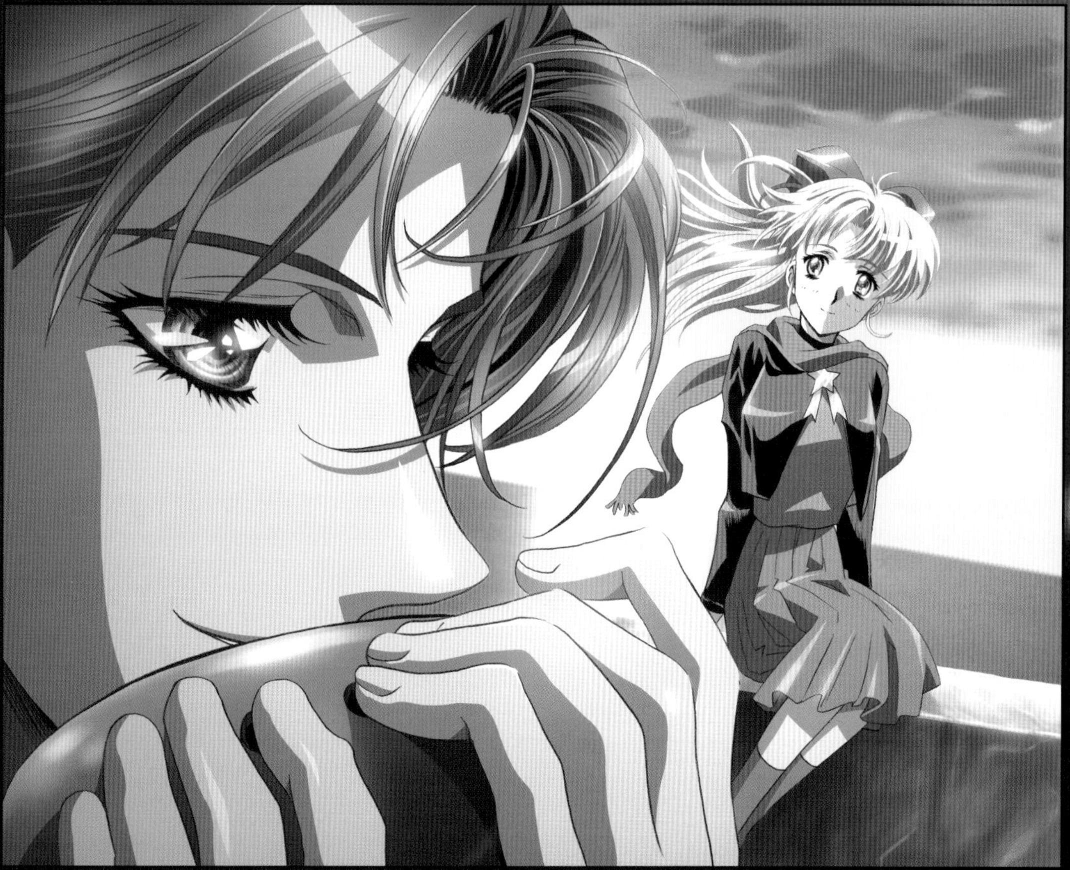

Yet, an accumulation of heartrending, fated occurrences would before long interfere and cause a shadow to darken the meeting between the girl, Nagisa Shion, and the ocarina flute-playing boy, Jun Mato. All existed purely as elements leading to the pillage and massacre of the "logic world."

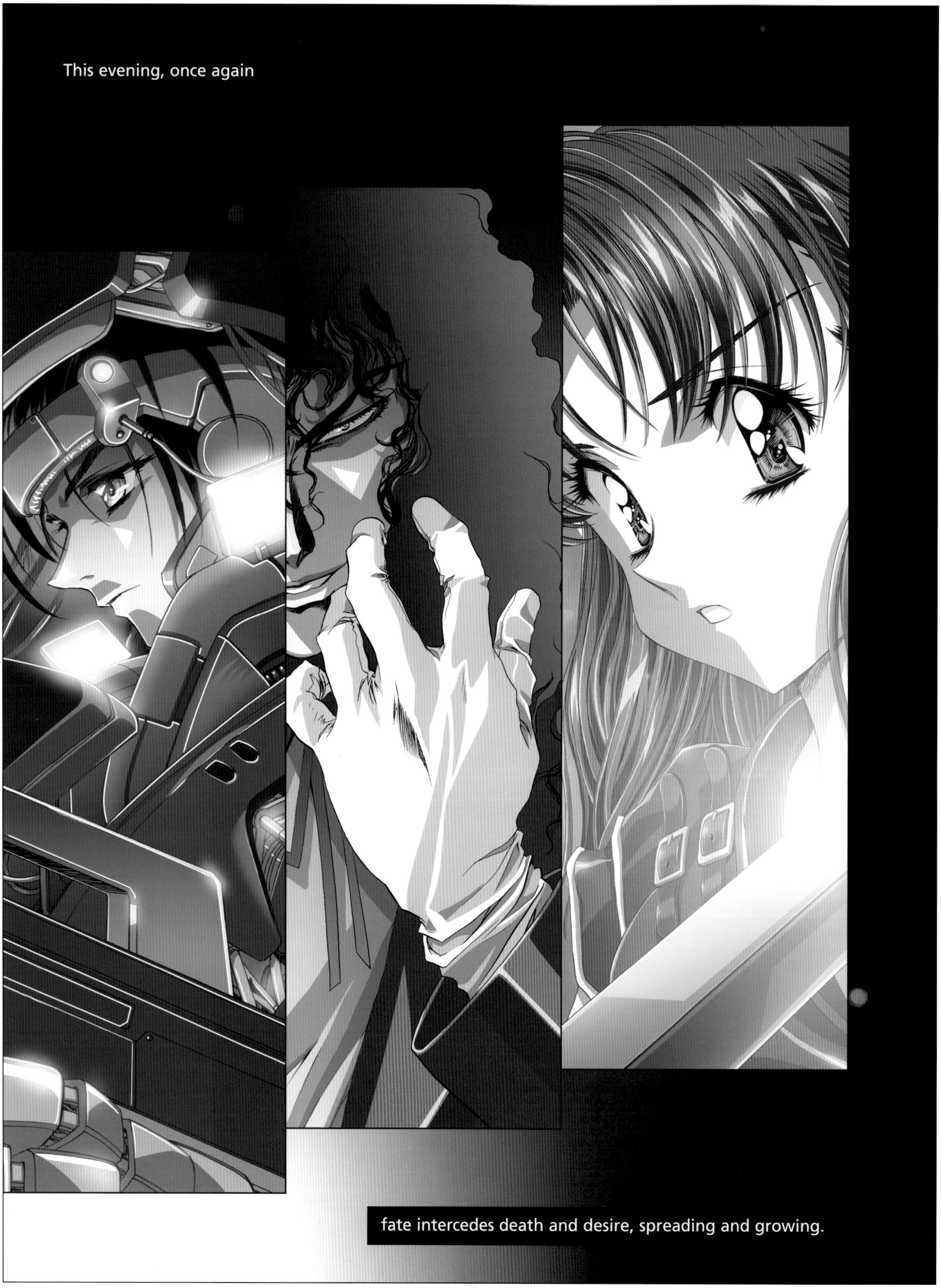
This evening, once again
fate intercedes death and desire, spreading and growing.

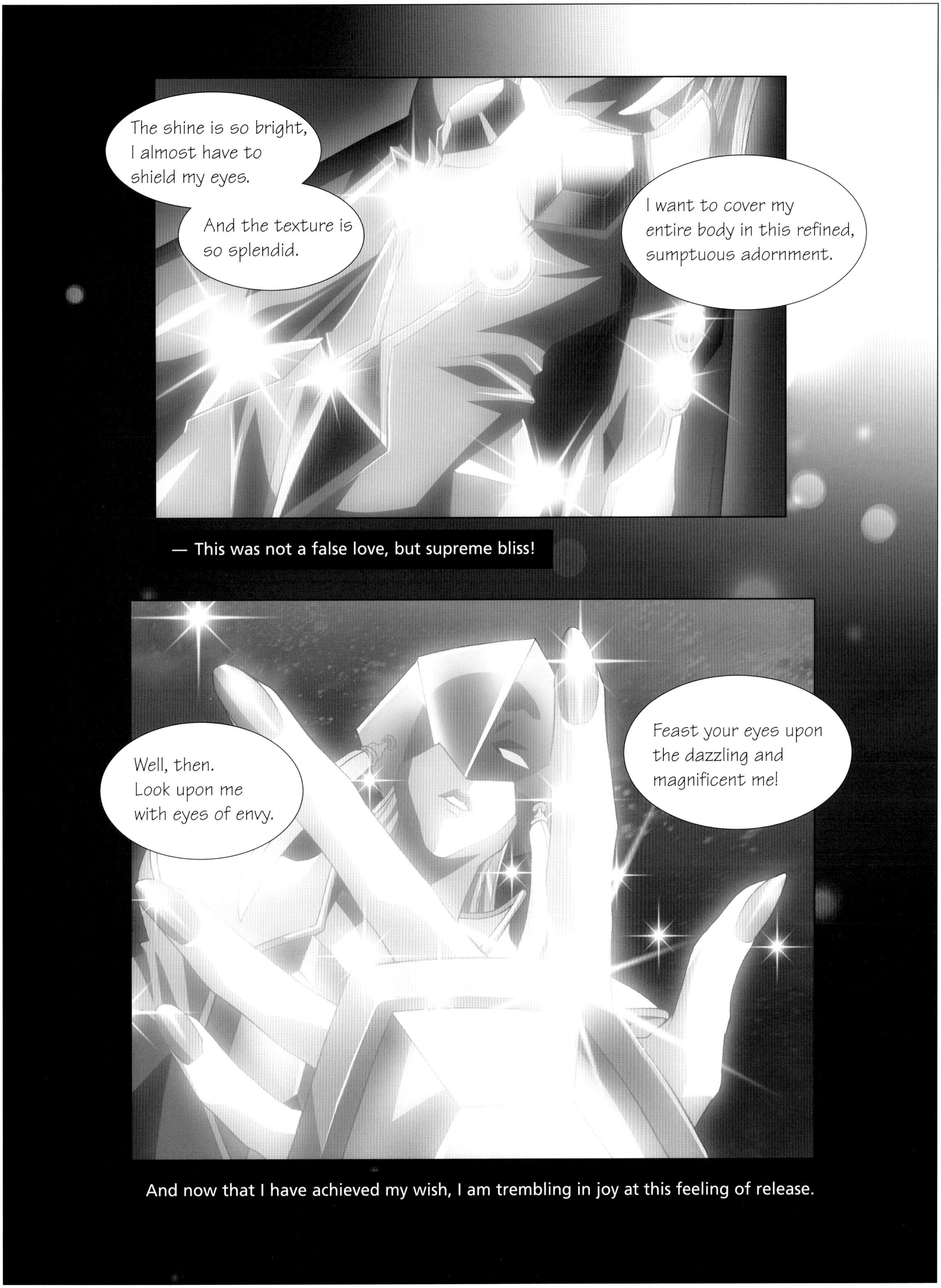
The shine is so bright, I almost have to shield my eyes.
And the texture is so splendid.
I want to cover my entire body in this refined, sumptuous adornment.
— This was not a false love, but supreme bliss!
Well, then. Look upon me with eyes of envy.
Feast your eyes upon the dazzling and magnificent me!
And now that I have achieved my wish, I am trembling in joy at this feeling of release.

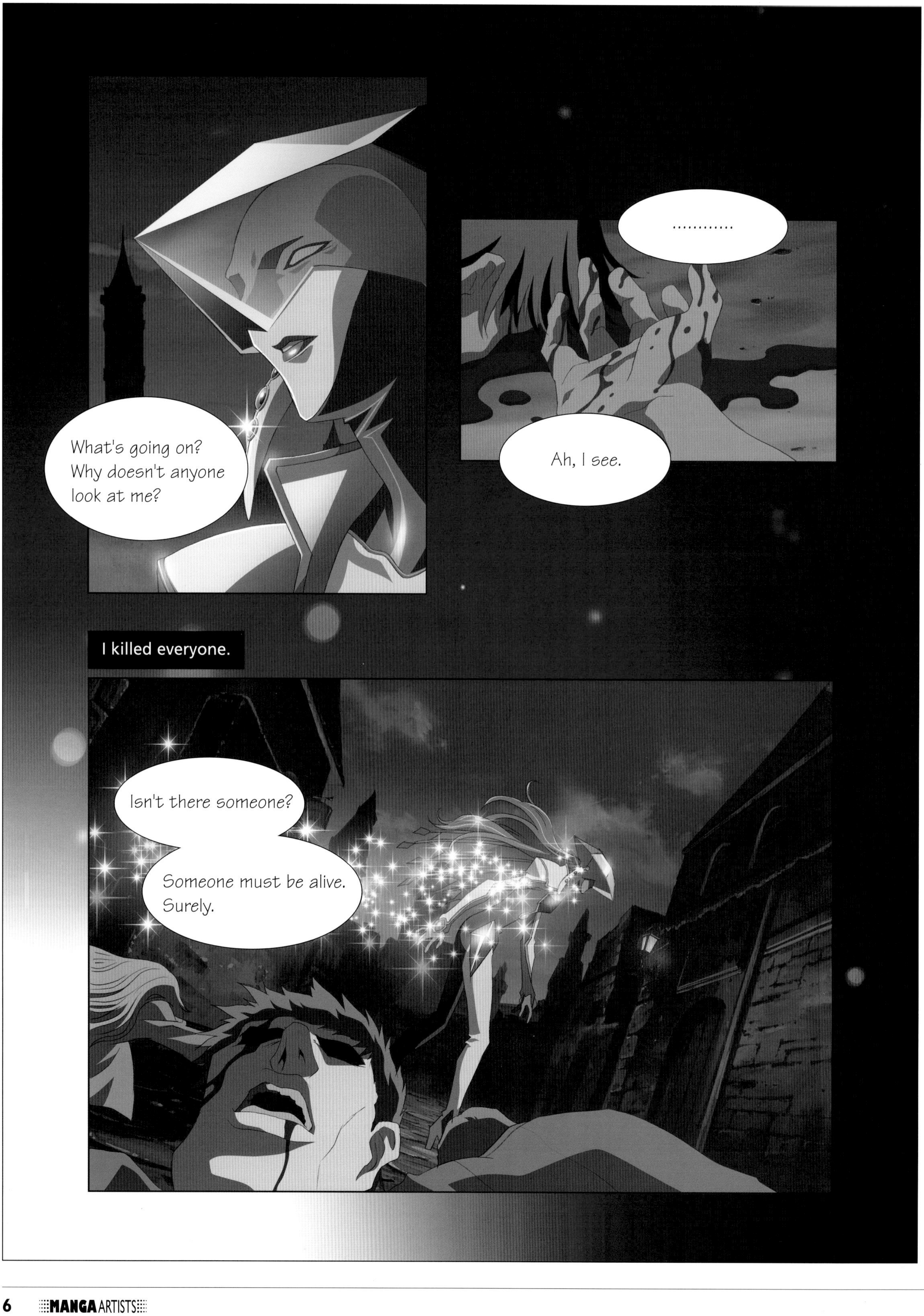
What's going on?
Why doesn't anyone look at me?
....
Ah, I see.
I killed everyone.
Isn't there someone?
Someone must be alive.
Surely.

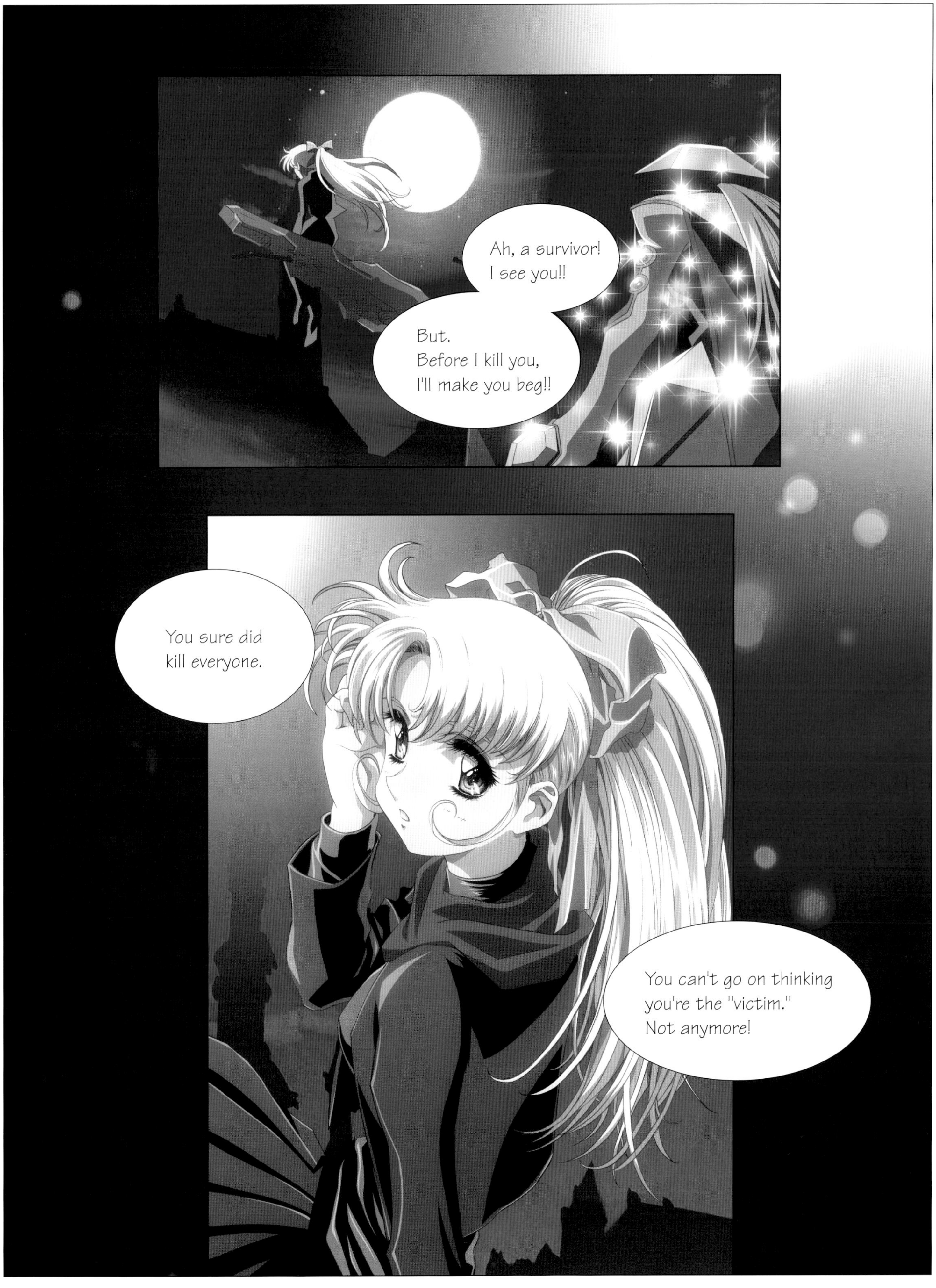
Ah, a survivor!
I see you!!
But.
Before I kill you,
I'll make you beg!!
You sure did kill everyone.
You can't go on thinking you're the "victim." Not anymore!

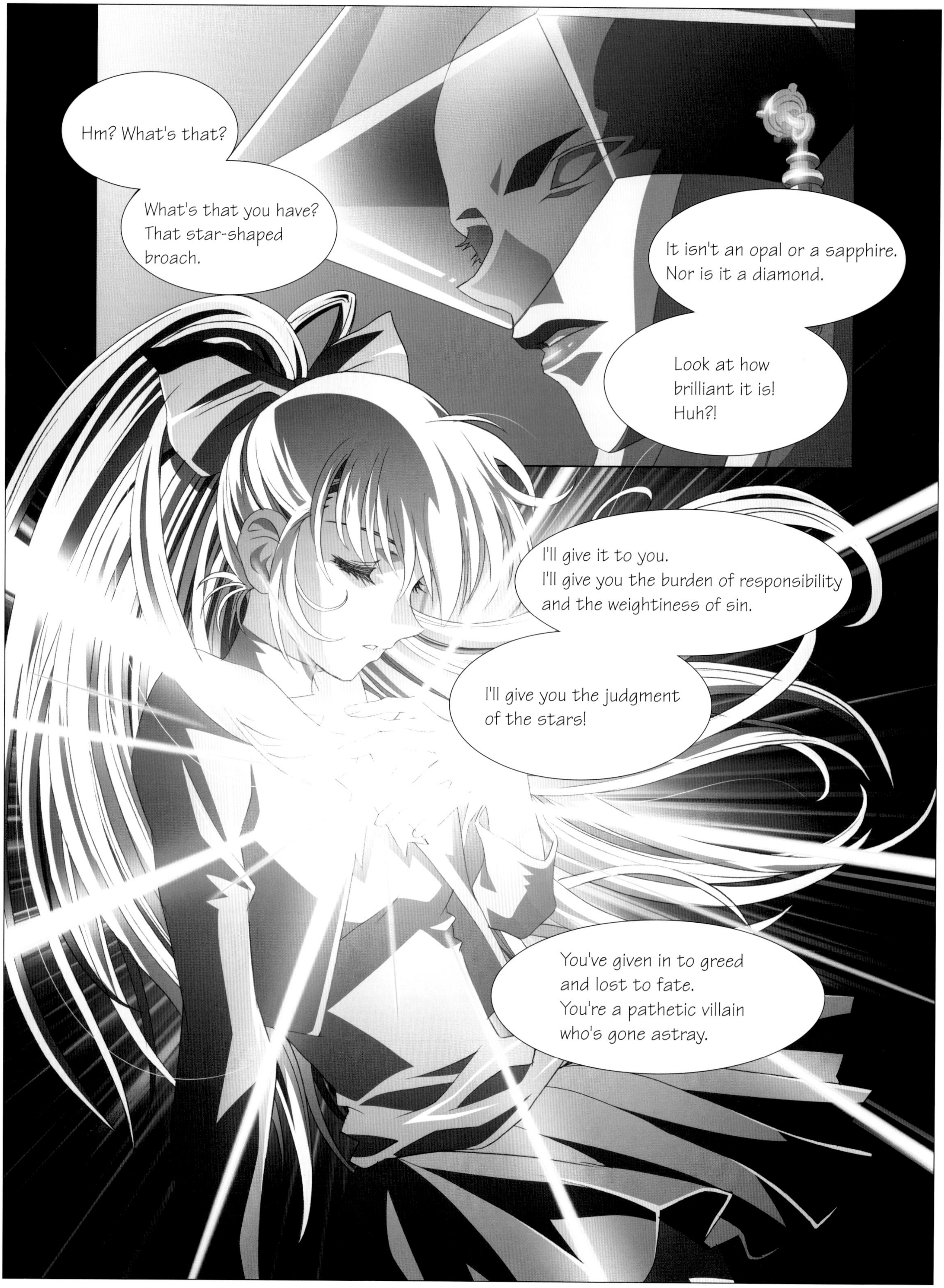
Hm? What's that?
What's that you have? That star-shaped broach.
It isn't an opal or a sapphire. Nor is it a diamond.
Look at how brilliant it is! Huh?!
I'll give it to you. I'll give you the burden of responsibility and the weightiness of sin.
I'll give you the judgment of the stars!
You've given in to greed and lost to fate. You're a pathetic villain who's gone astray.

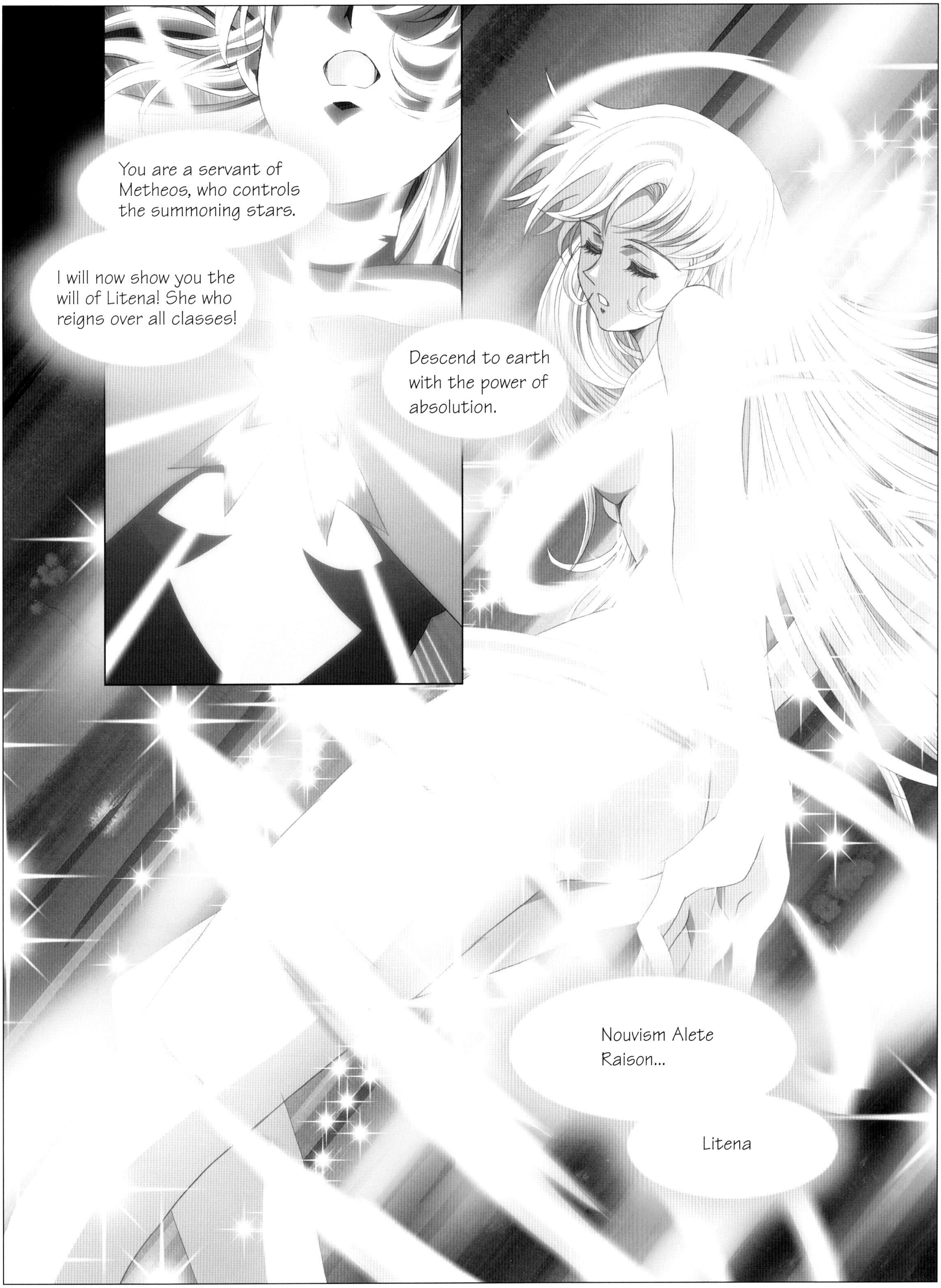
You are a servant of Metheos, who controls the summoning stars.
I will now show you the will of Litena! She who reigns over all classes!
Descend to earth with the power of absolution.
Nouvism Alete Raison...
Litena

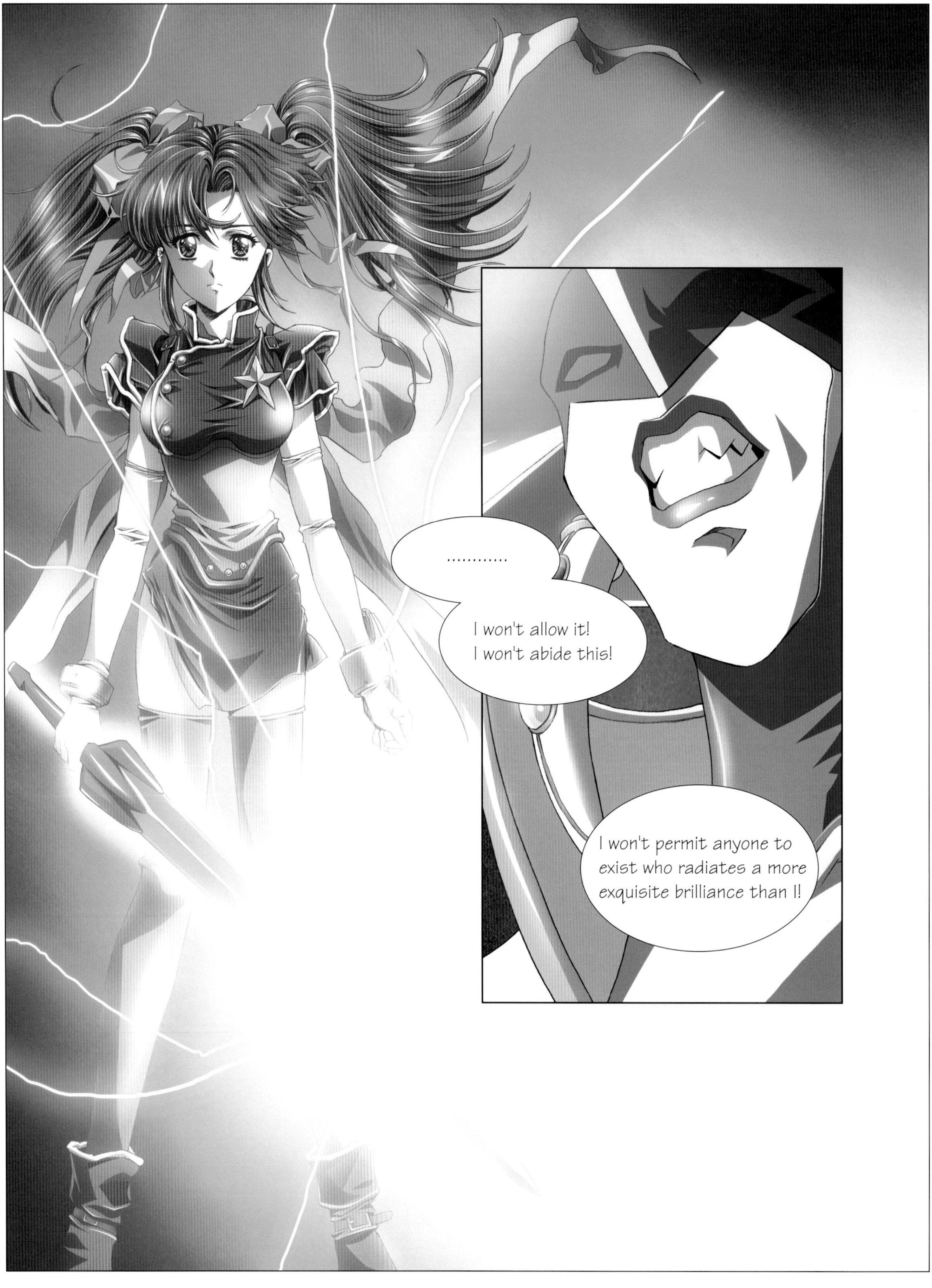
....
I won't allow it!
I won't abide this!
I won't permit anyone to exist who radiates a more exquisite brilliance than I!

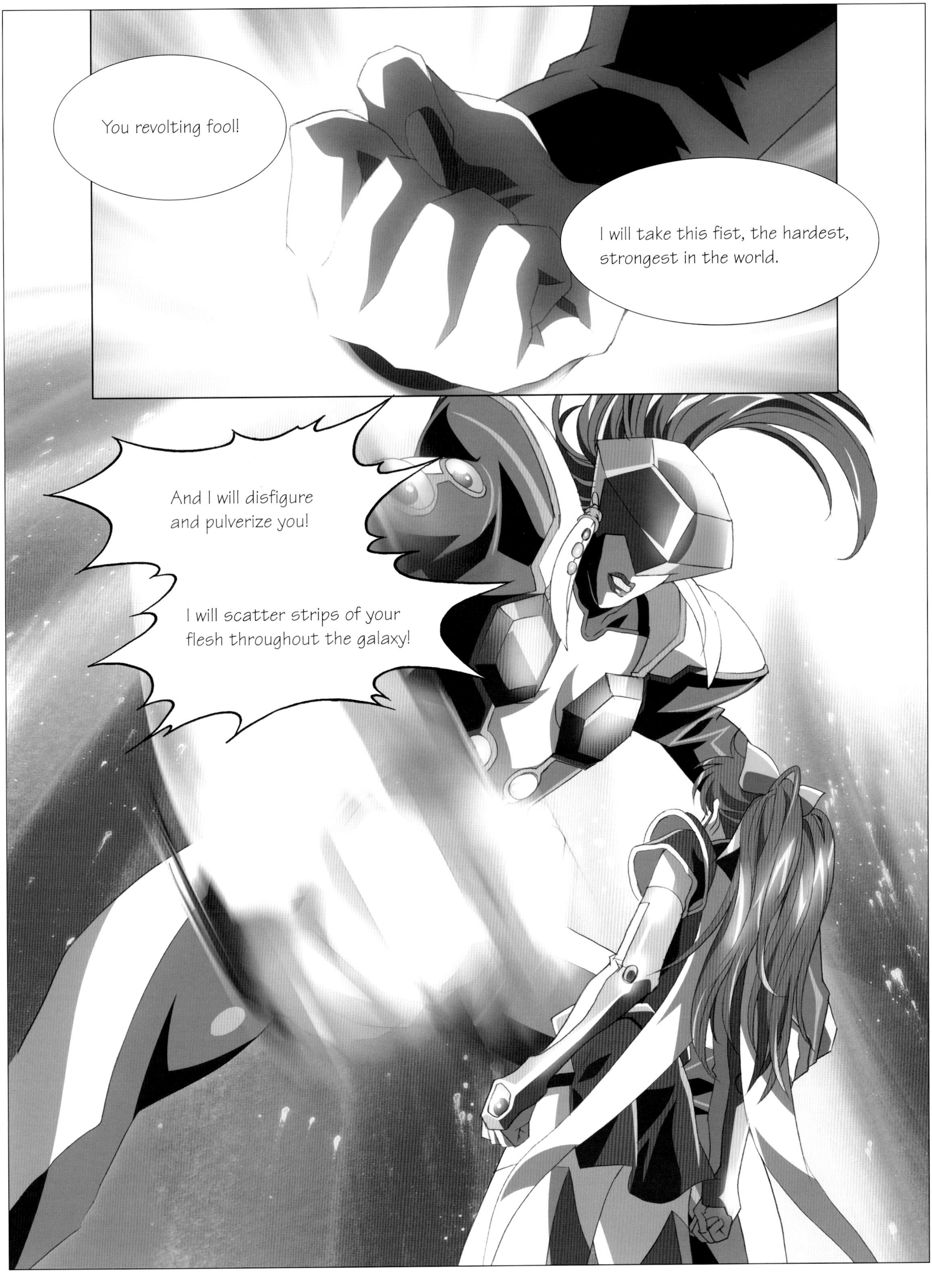
You revolting fool!
I will take this fist, the hardest, strongest in the world.
And I will disfigure and pulverize you!
I will scatter strips of your flesh throughout the galaxy!

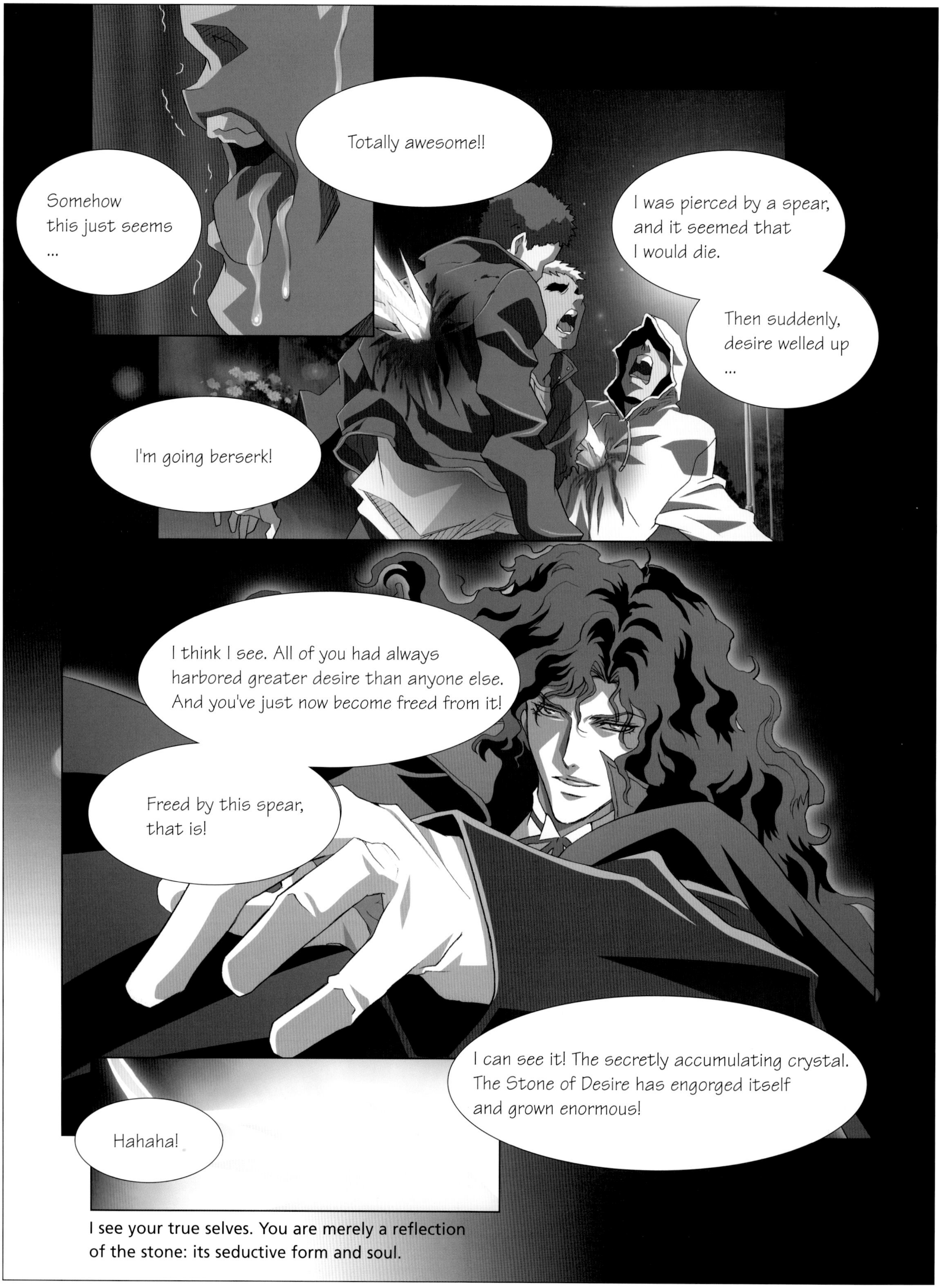
Totally awesome!!
Somehow this just seems ...
I was pierced by a spear, and it seemed that I would die.
Then suddenly, desire welled up ...
I'm going berserk!
I think I see. All of you had always harbored greater desire than anyone else. And you've just now become freed from it!
Freed by this spear, that is!
I can see it! The secretly accumulating crystal. The Stone of Desire has engorged itself and grown enormous!
Hahaha!

I see your true selves. You are merely a reflection of the stone: its seductive form and soul.

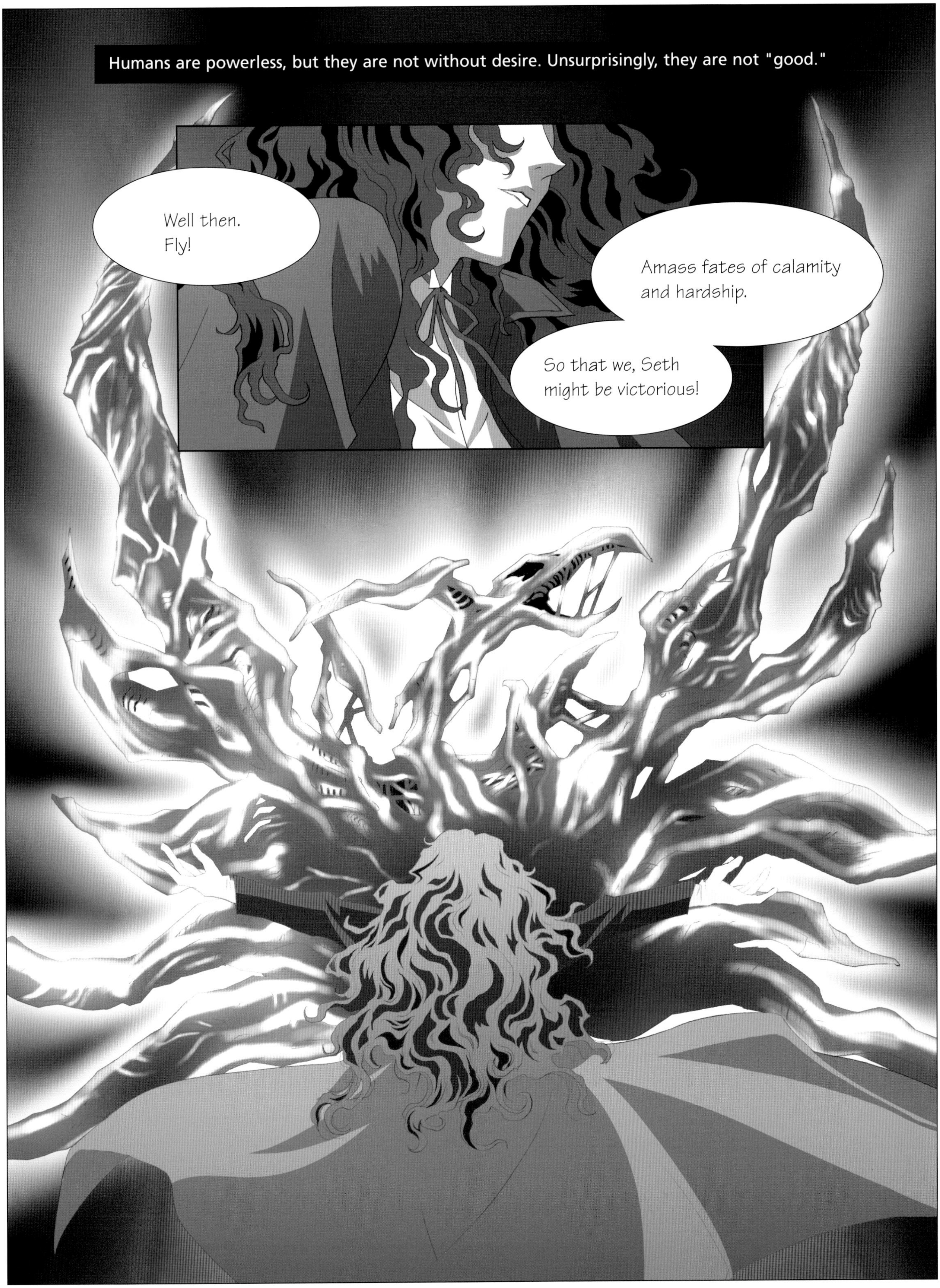
Humans are powerless, but they are not without desire. Unsurprisingly, they are not "good."
Well then. Fly!
Amass fates of calamity and hardship.
So that we, Seth might be victorious!

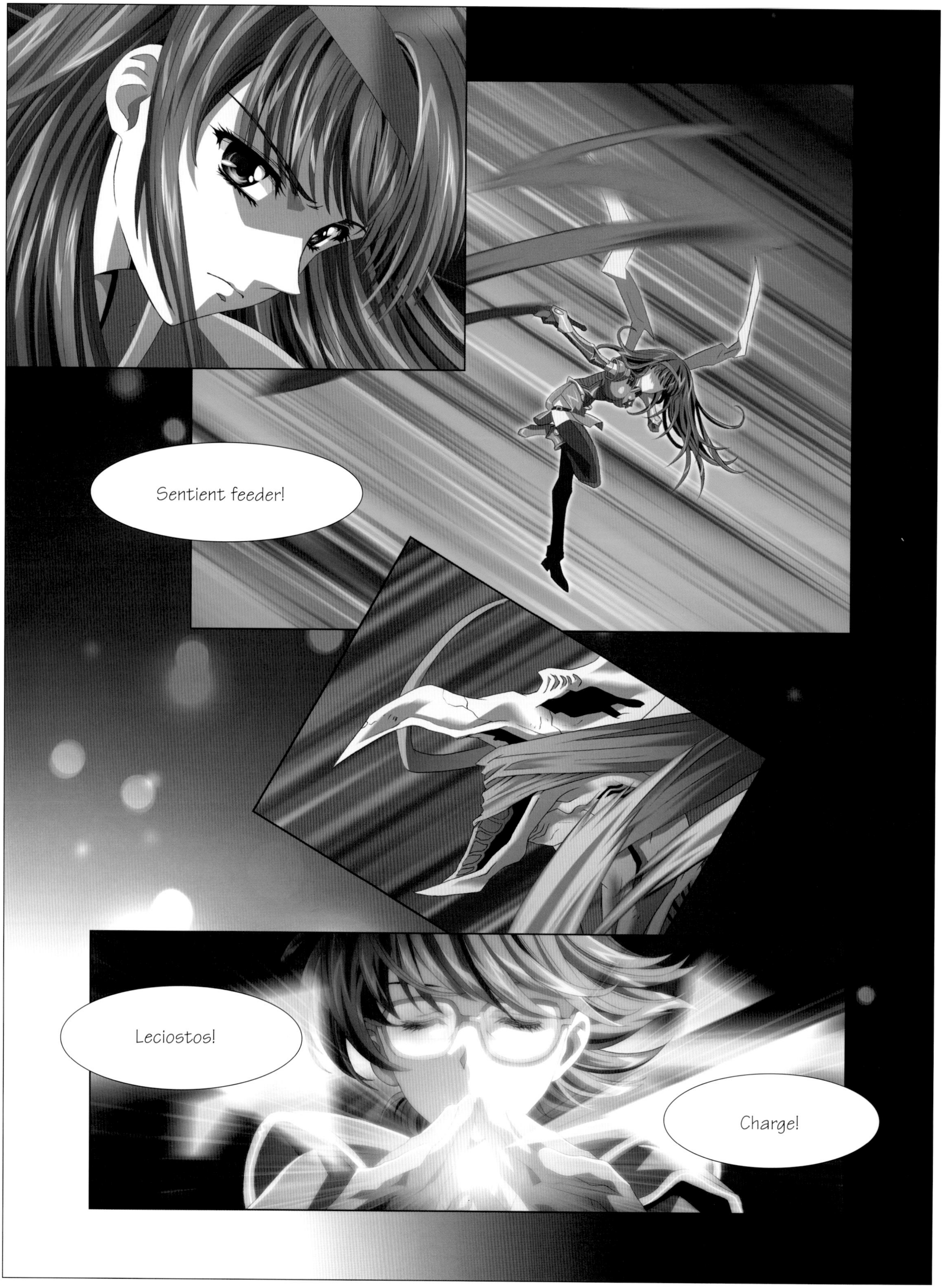
Sentient feeder!
Leciostos!
Charge!

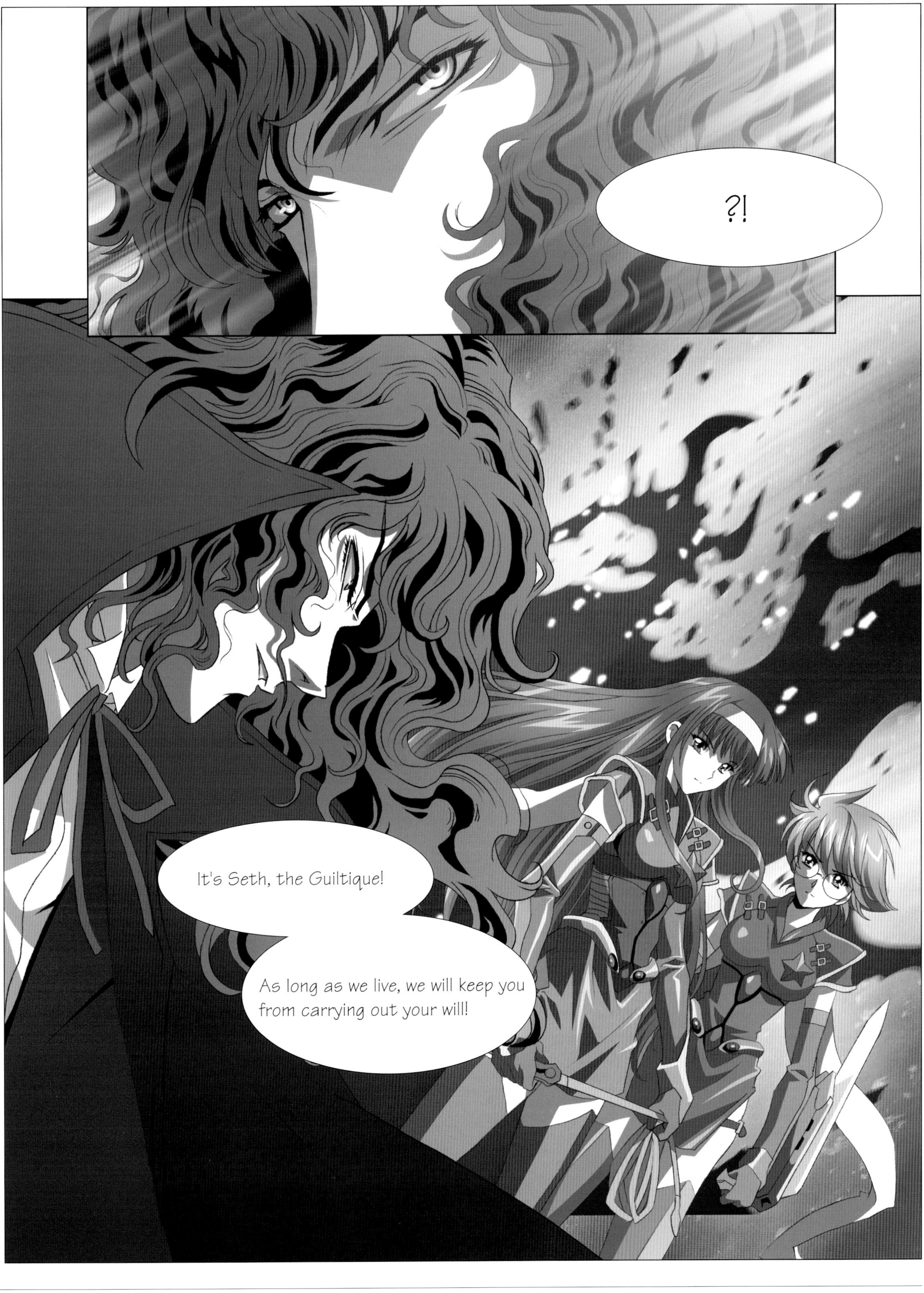
?!
It's Seth, the Guiltique!
As long as we live, we will keep you from carrying out your will!

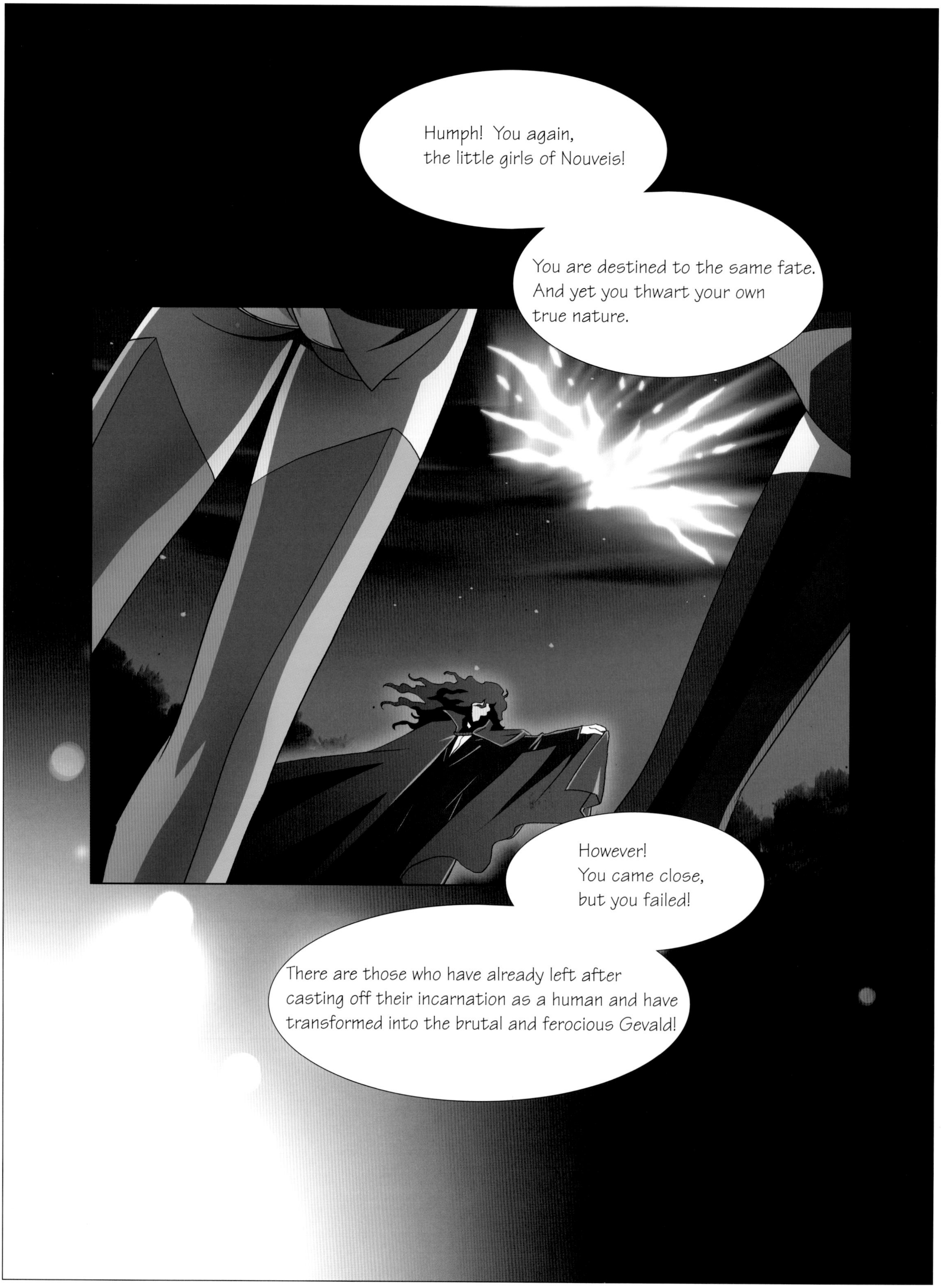
Humph! You again, the little girls of Nouveis!
You are destined to the same fate. And yet you thwart your own true nature.
However! You came close, but you failed!
There are those who have already left after casting off their incarnation as a human and have transformed into the brutal and ferocious Gevald!

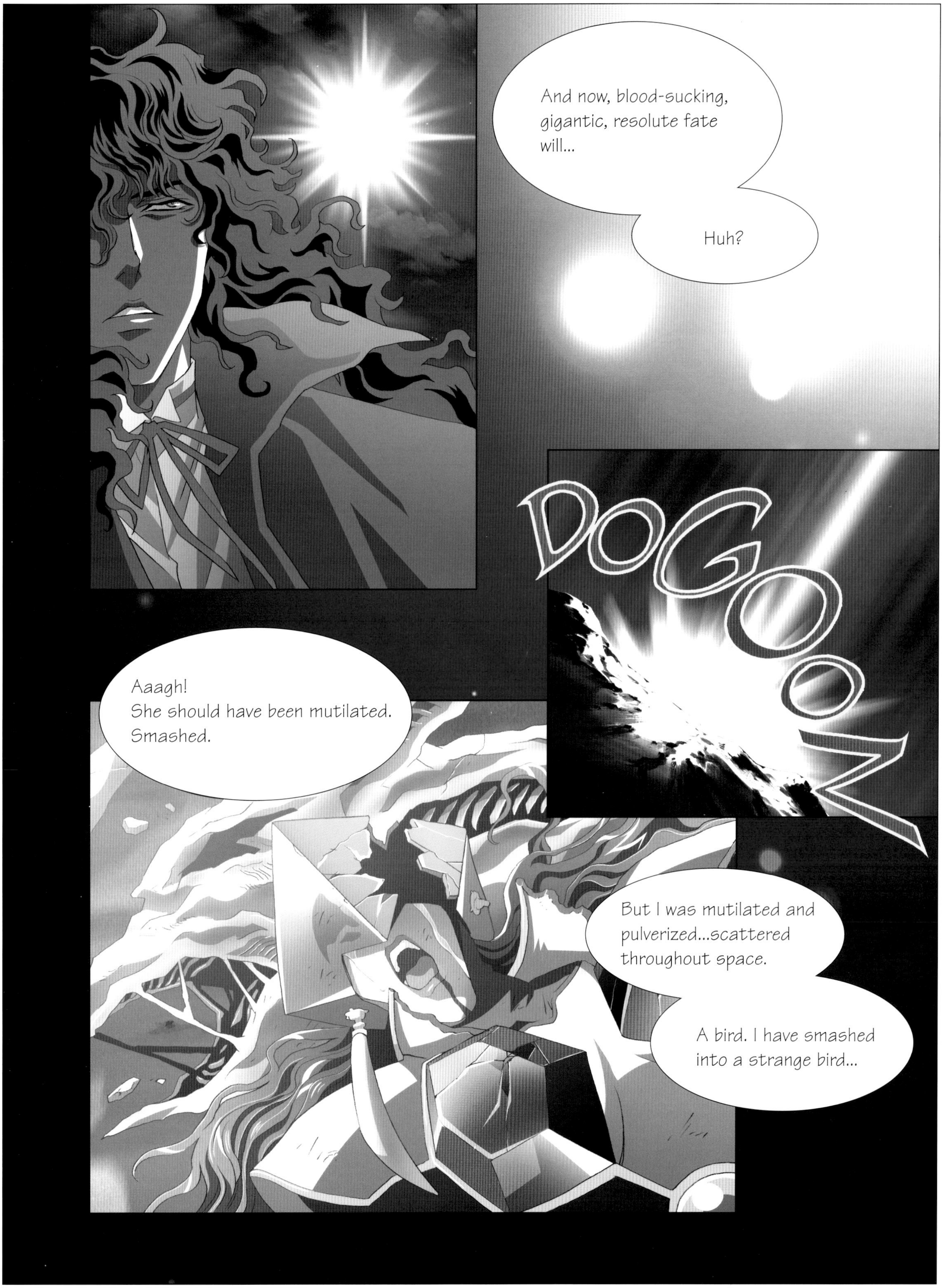
And now, blood-sucking, gigantic, resolute fate will...
Huh?
DOGOOON
Aaagh!
She should have been mutilated.
Smashed.
But I was mutilated and pulverized...scattered throughout space.
A bird. I have smashed into a strange bird...

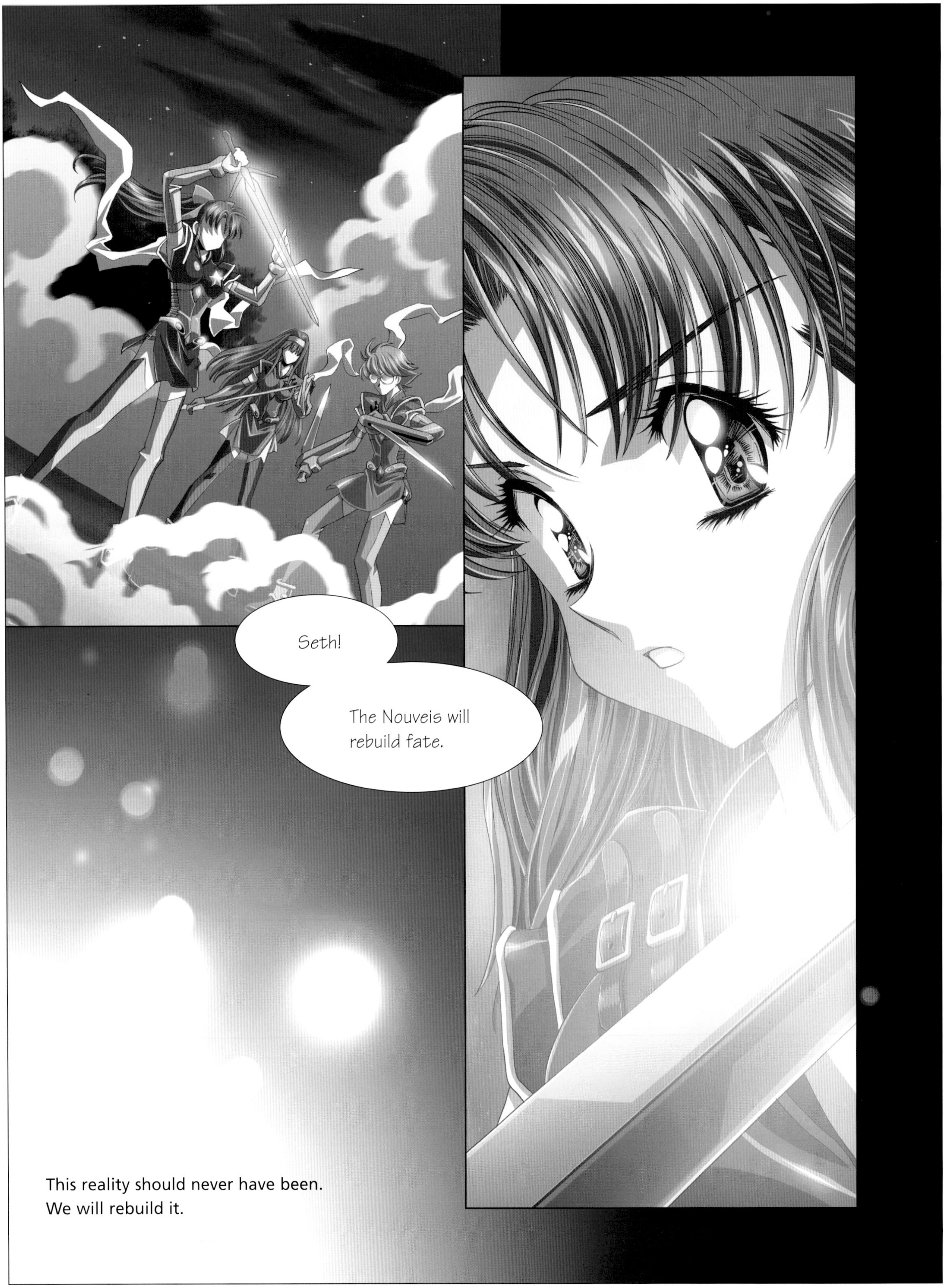
Seth!
The Nouveis will rebuild fate.
This reality should never have been. We will rebuild it.

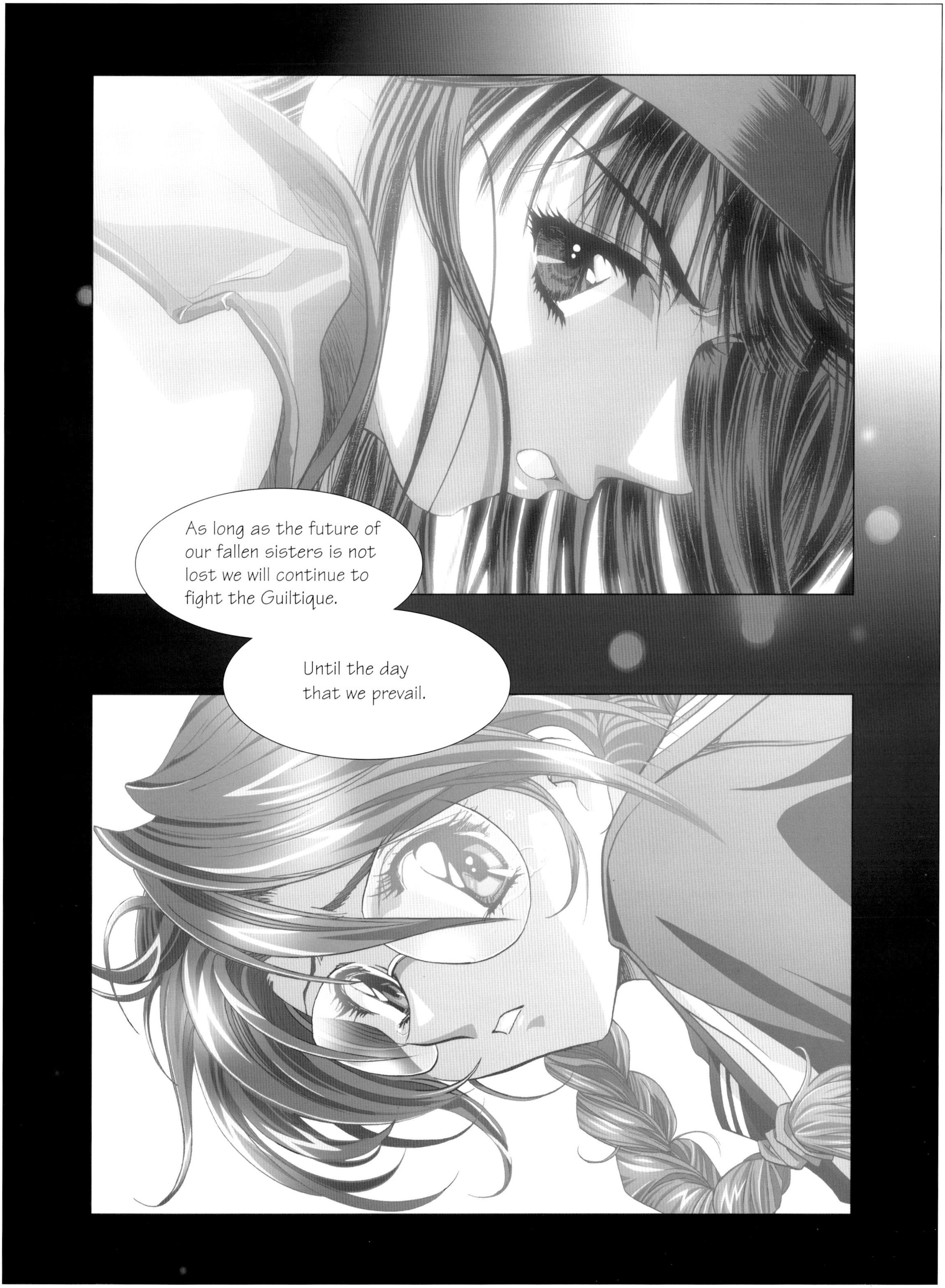
As long as the future of our fallen sisters is not lost we will continue to fight the Guiltique.
Until the day that we prevail.

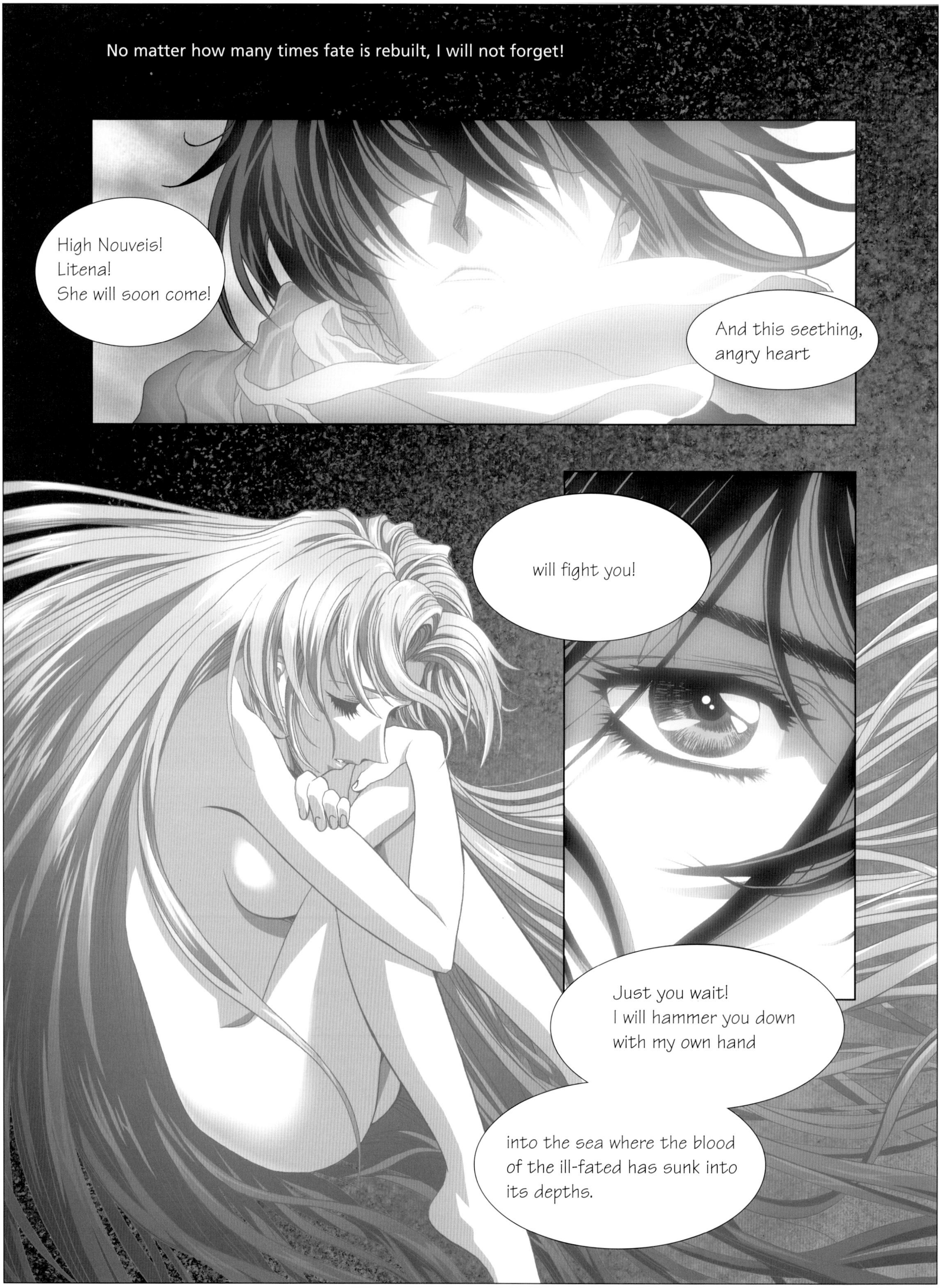
No matter how many times fate is rebuilt, I will not forget!
High Nouveis! Litena! She will soon come!
And this seething, angry heart
will fight you!
Just you wait! I will hammer you down with my own hand
into the sea where the blood of the ill-fated has sunk into its depths.

NOUVEIS LOGIC

Illustration Collection

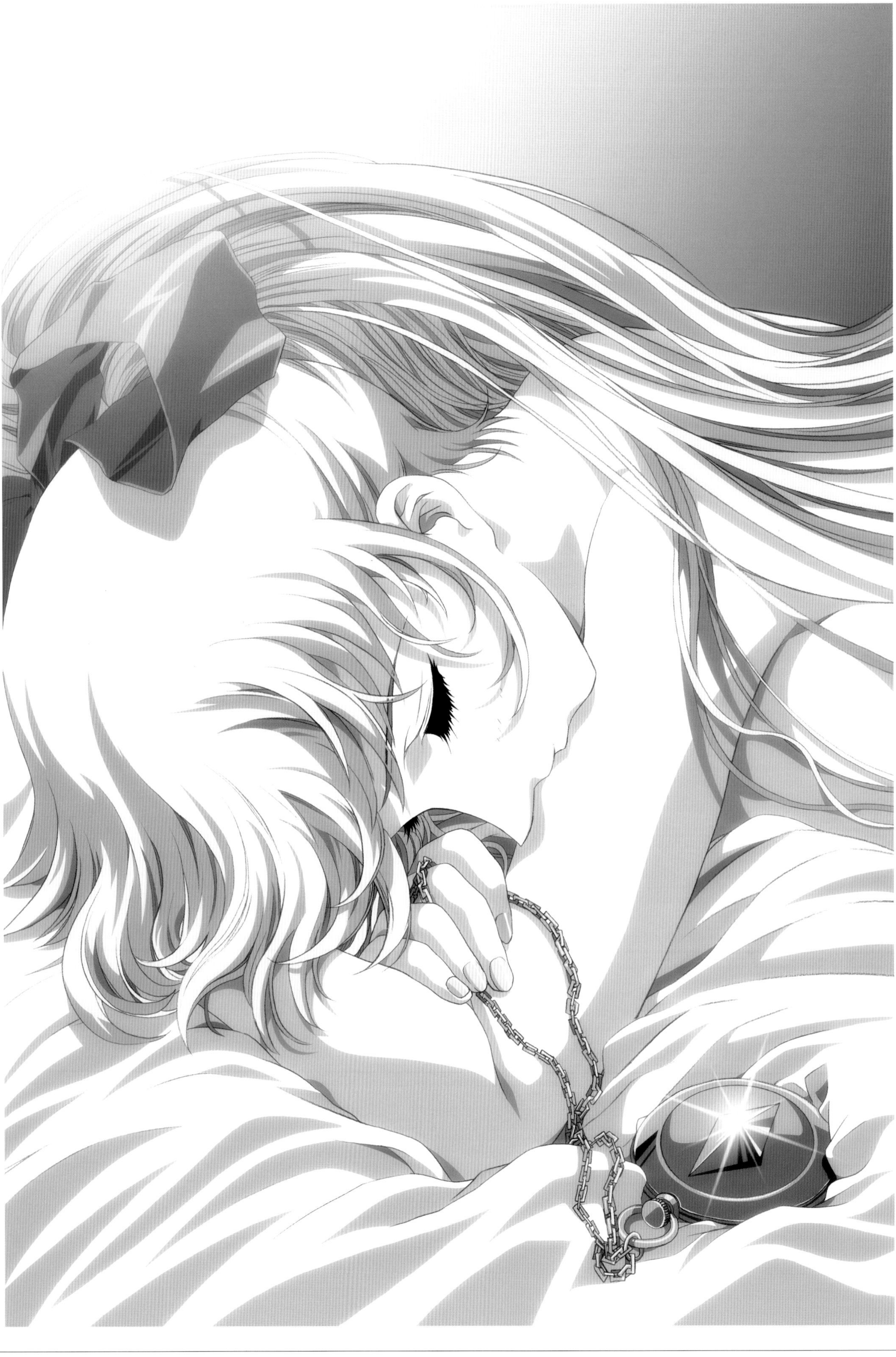

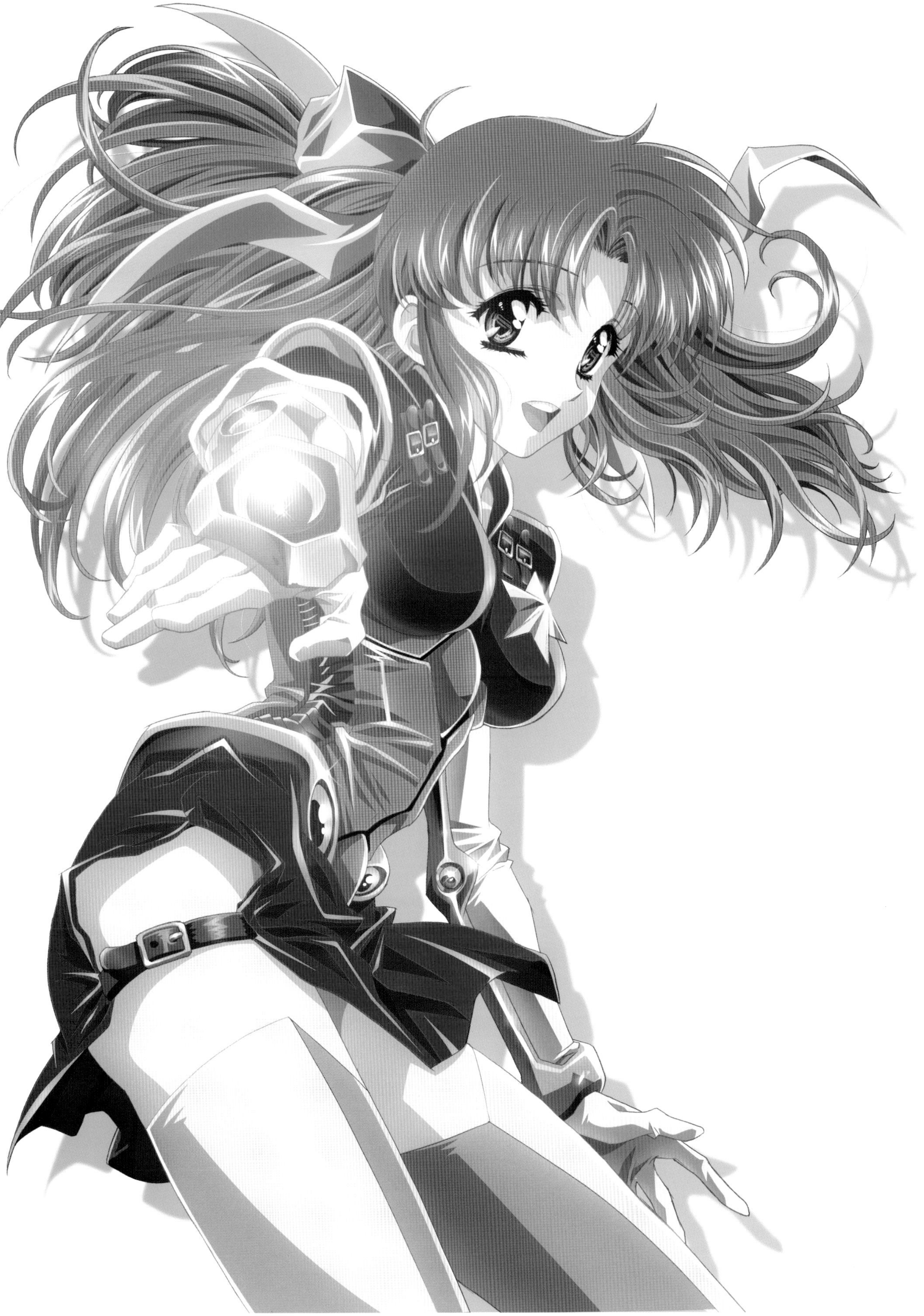

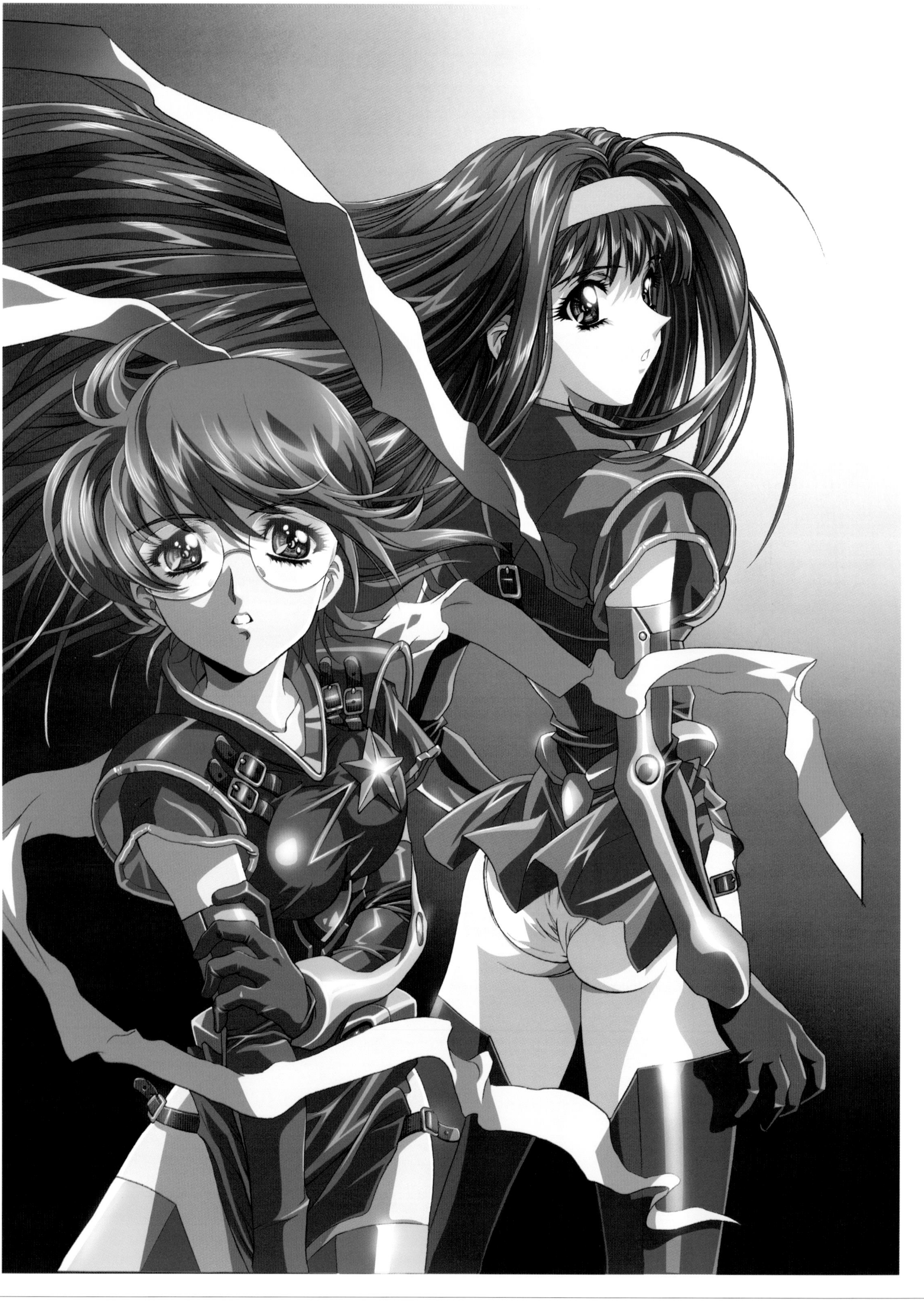

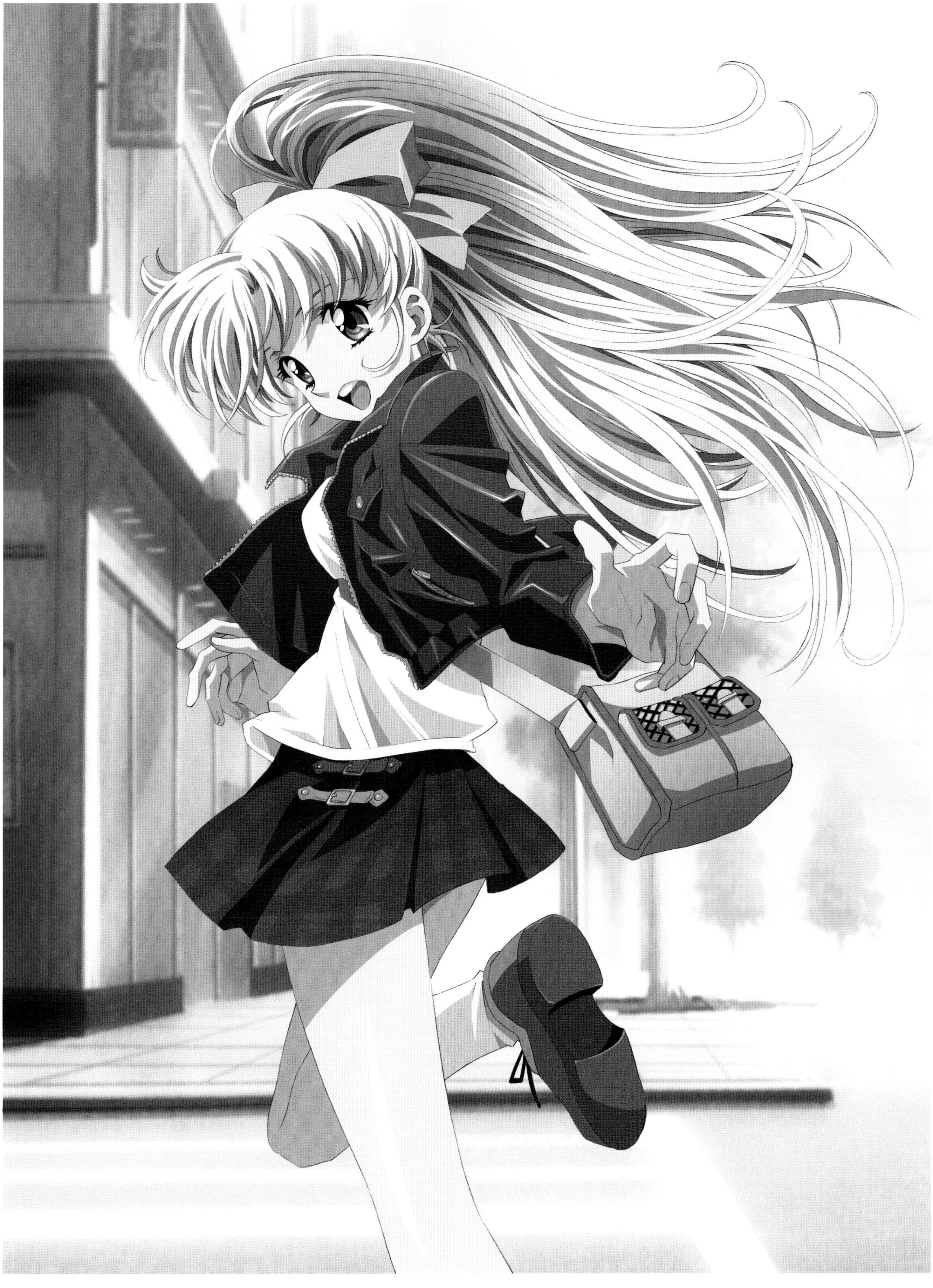

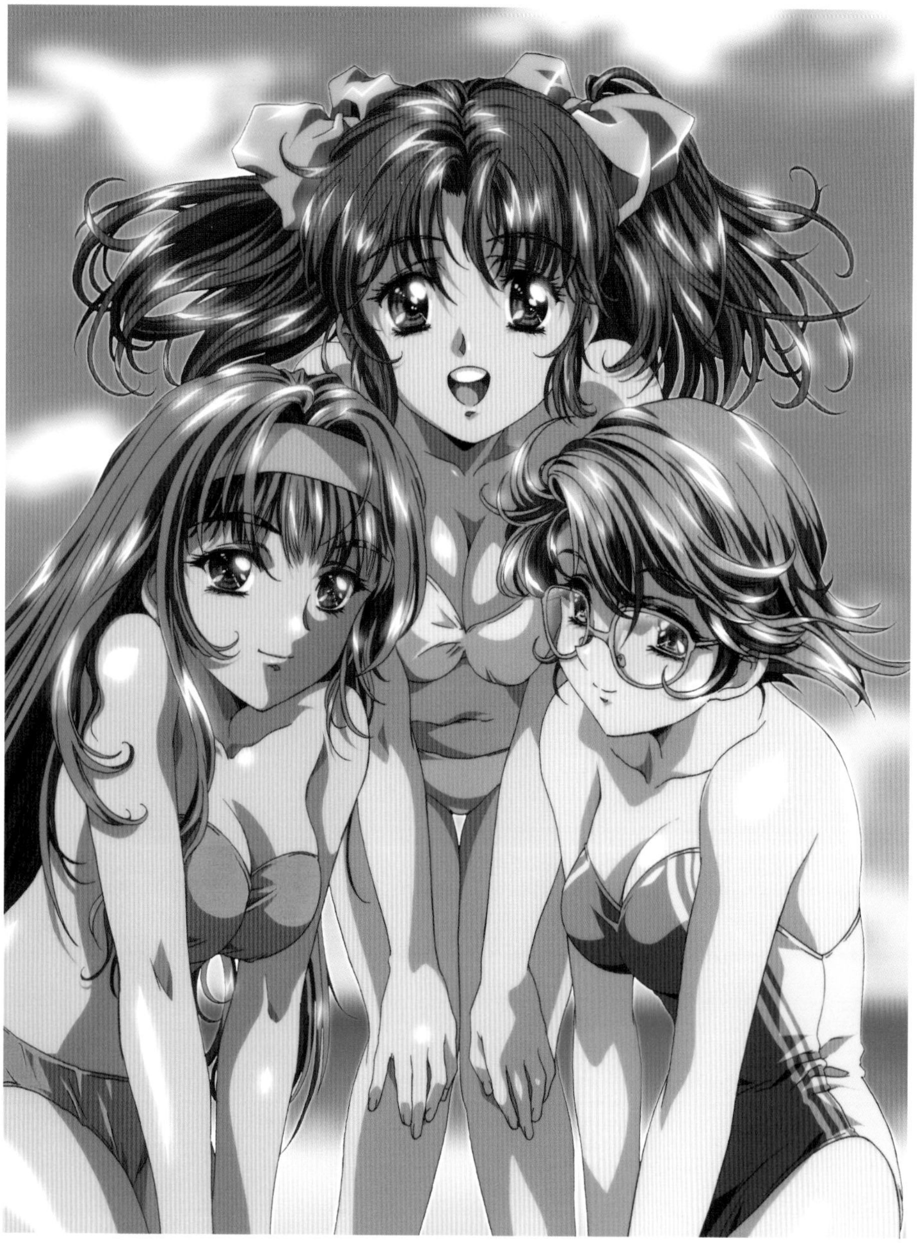

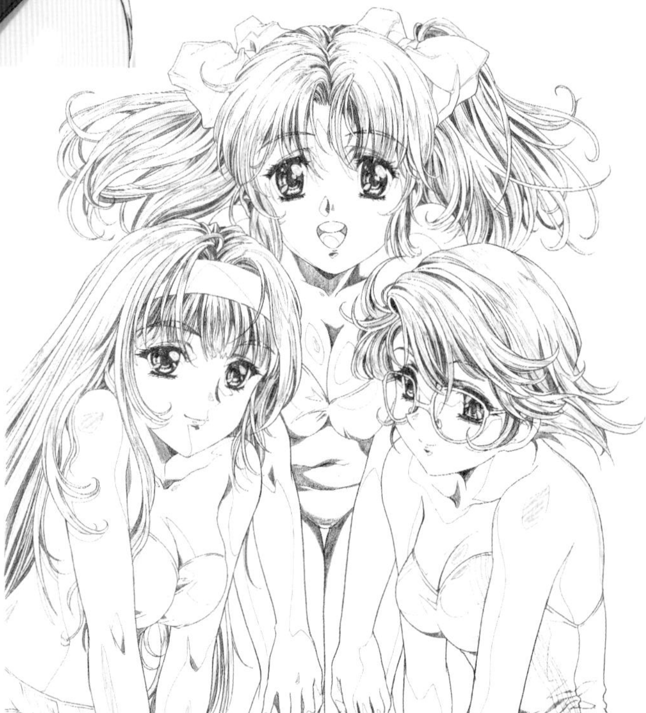

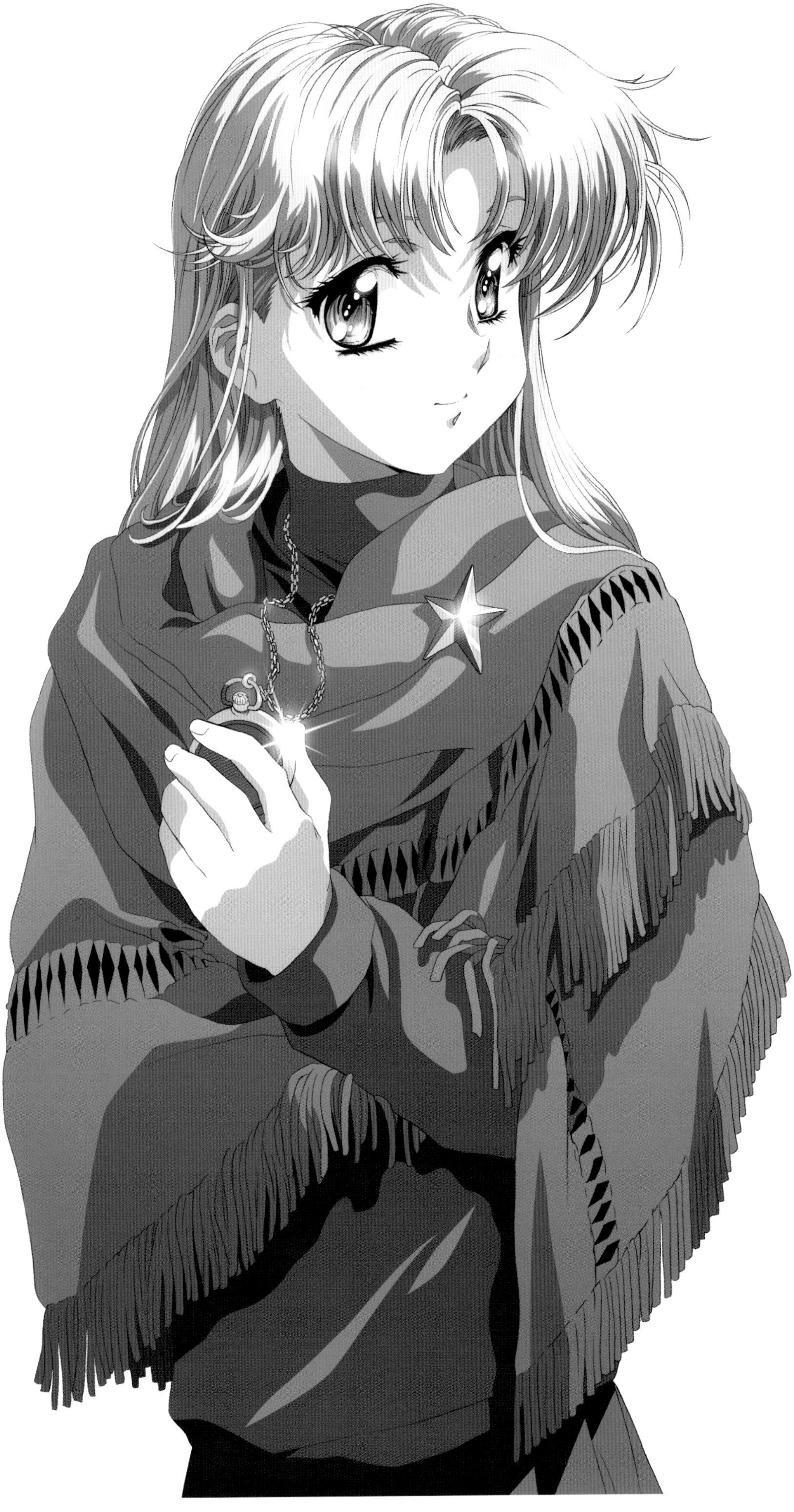

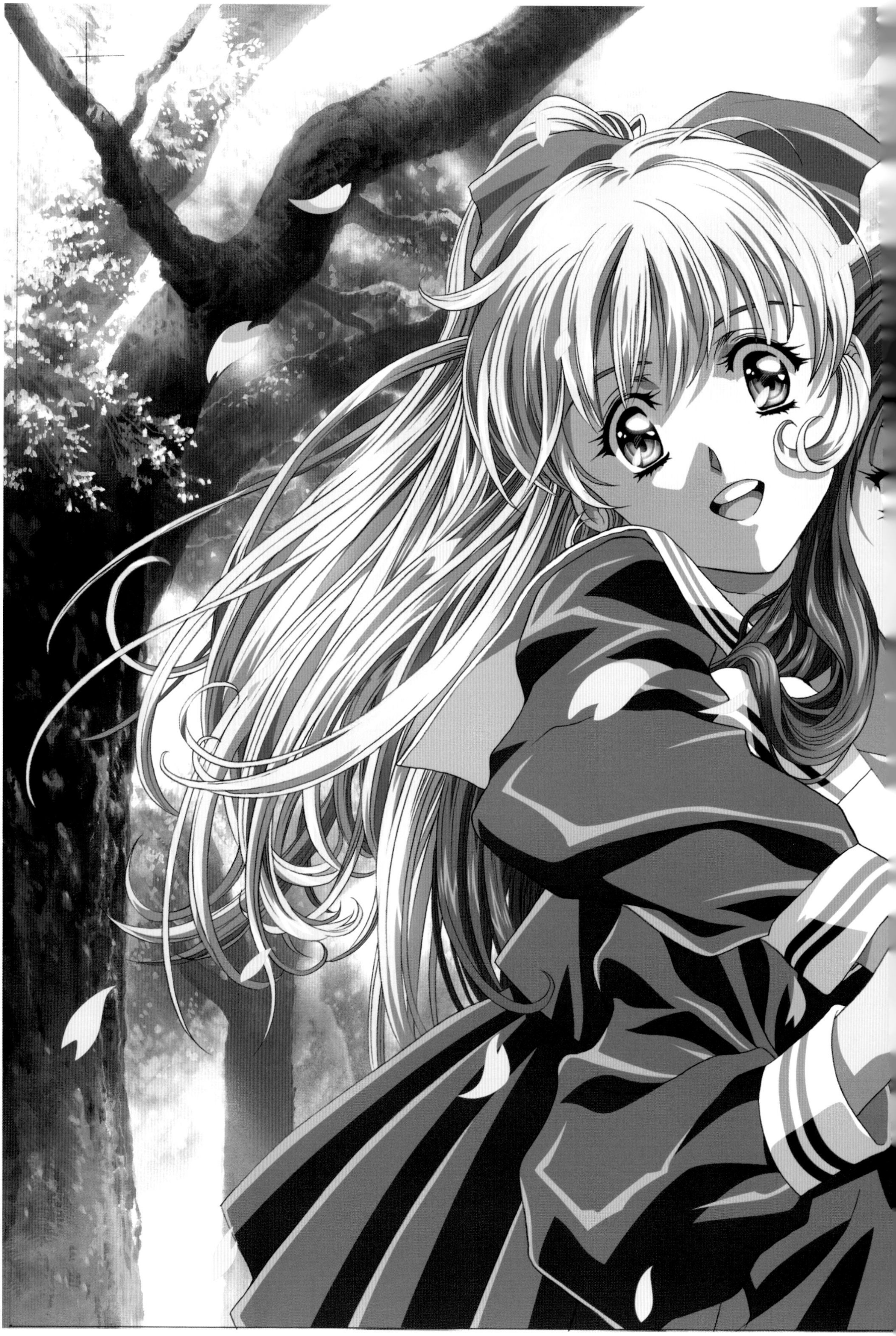

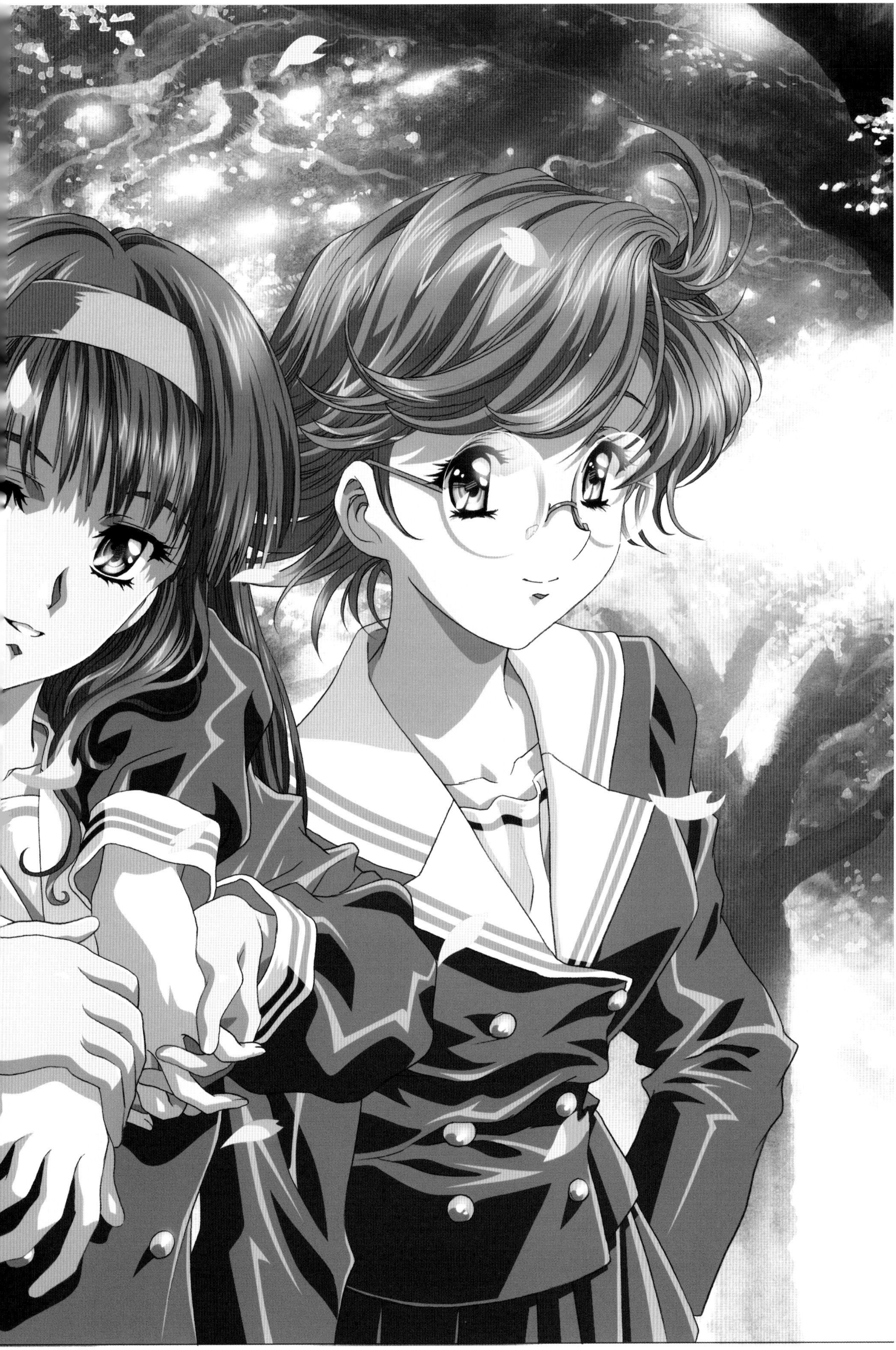

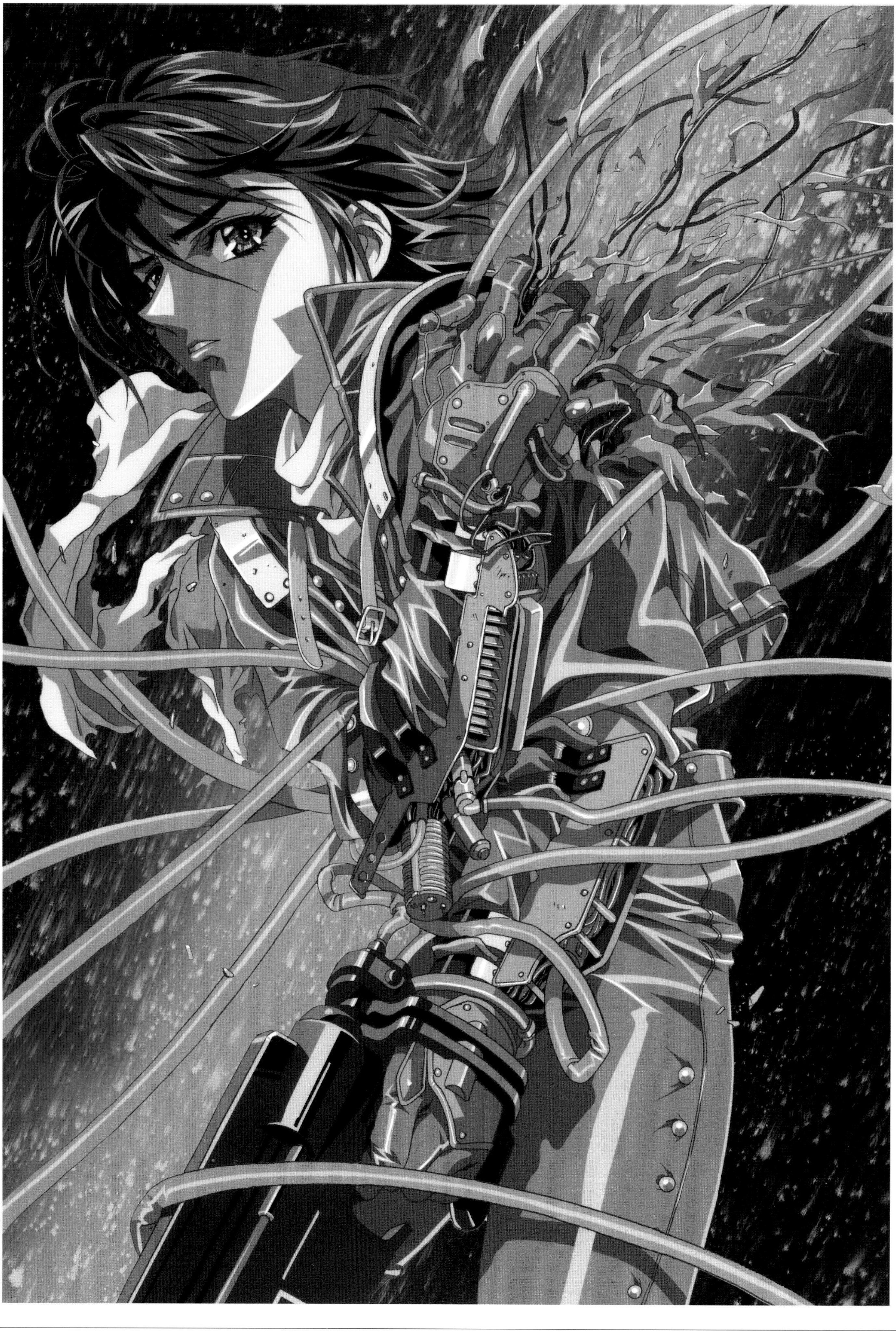

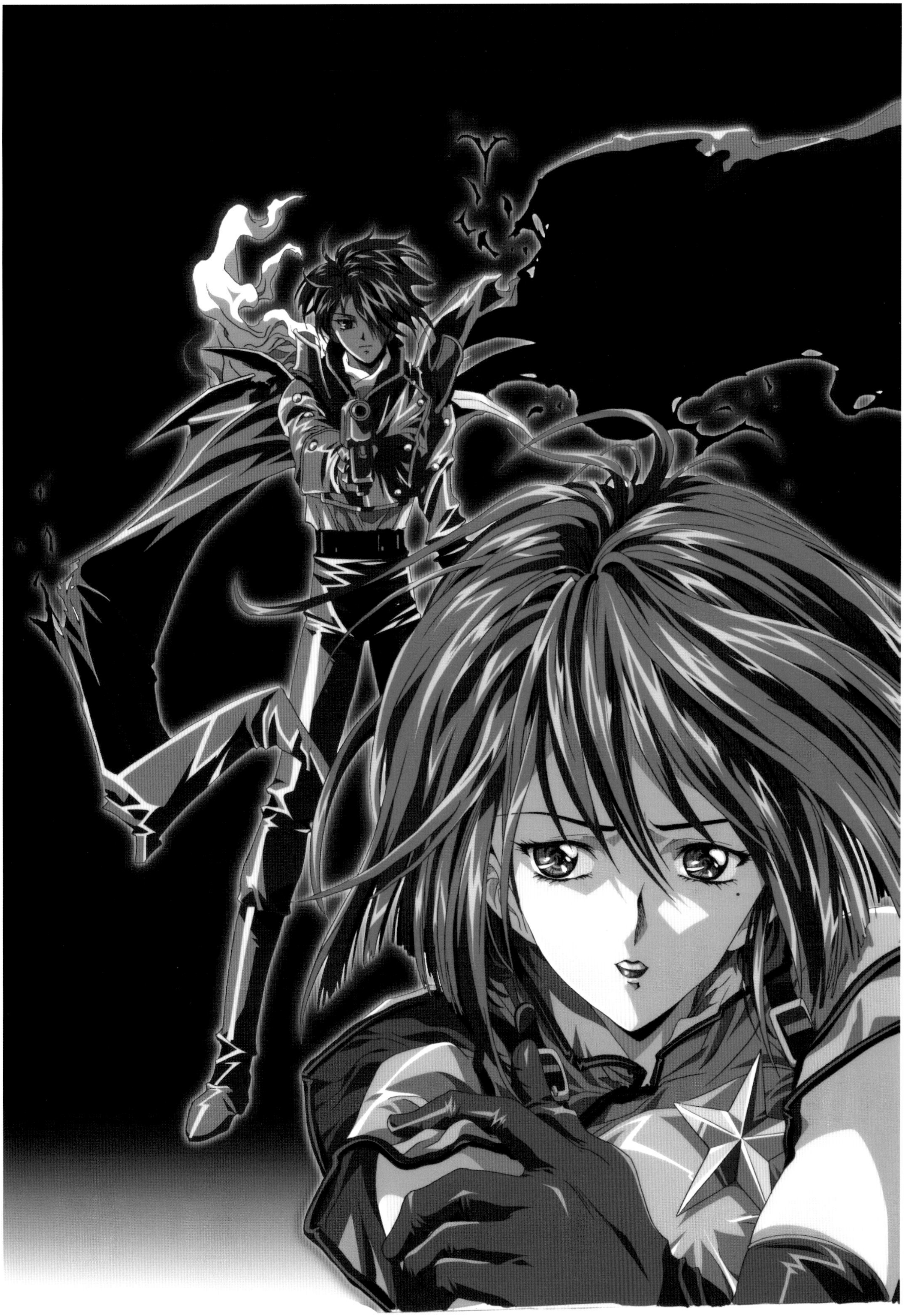

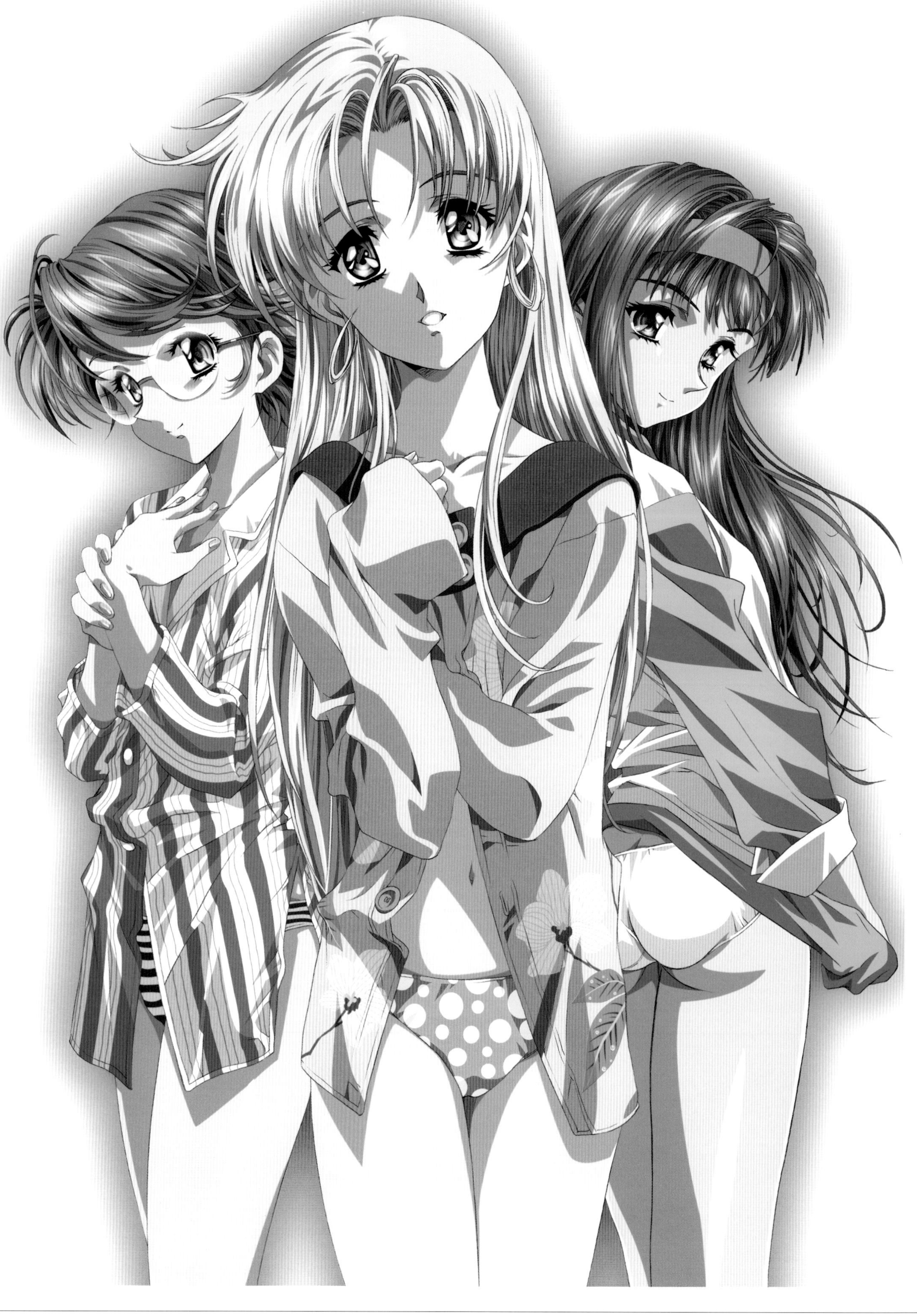

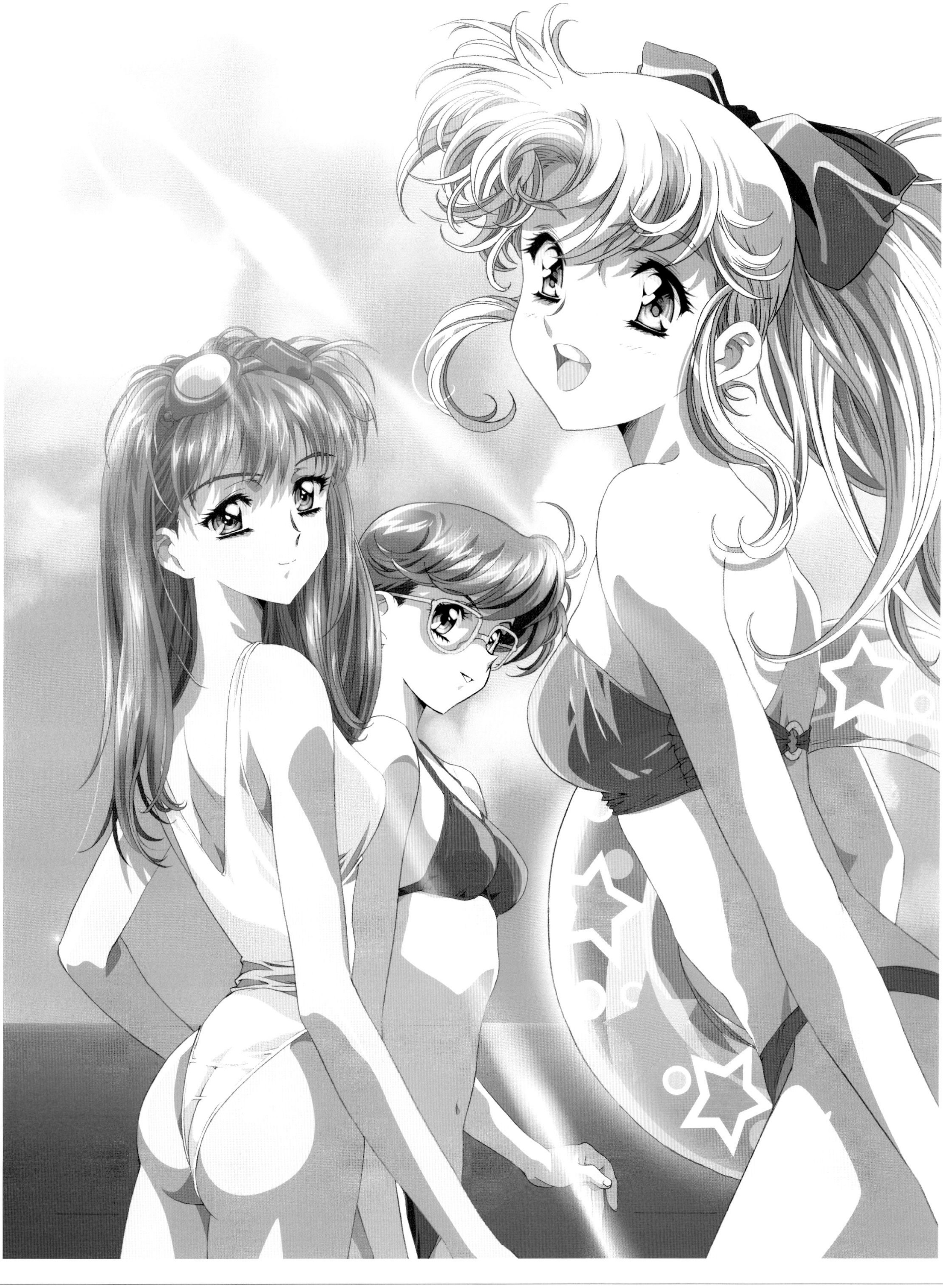

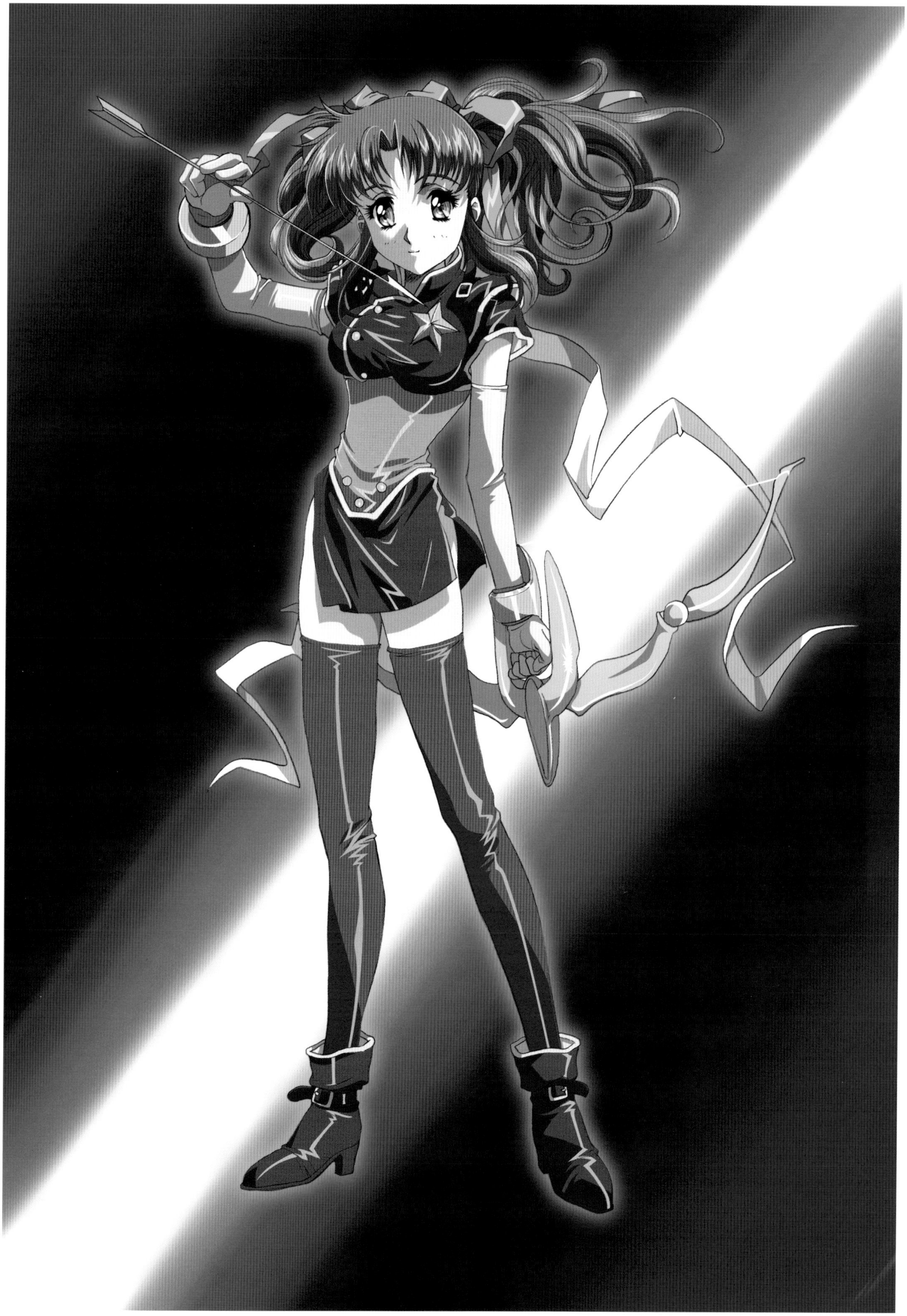

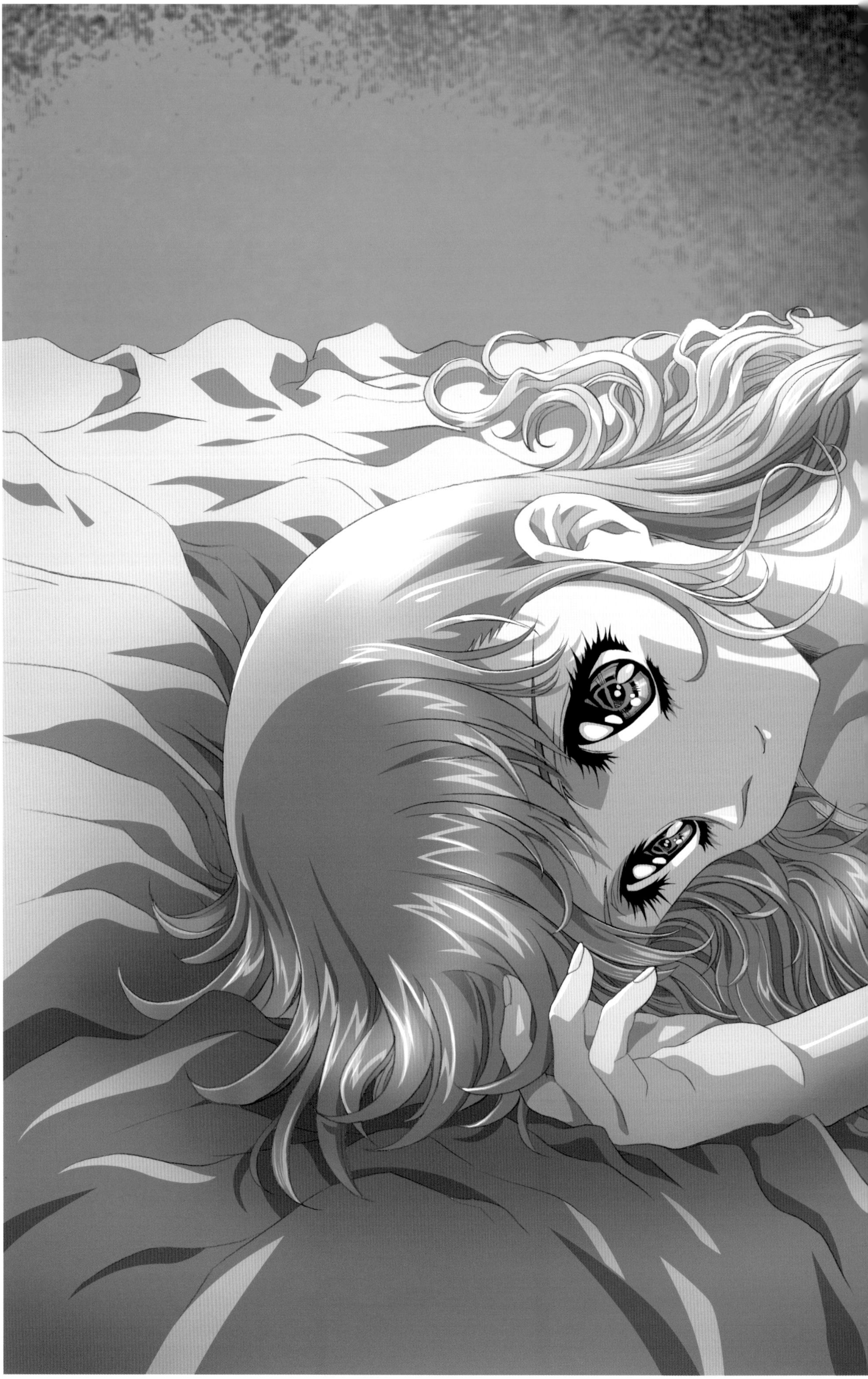

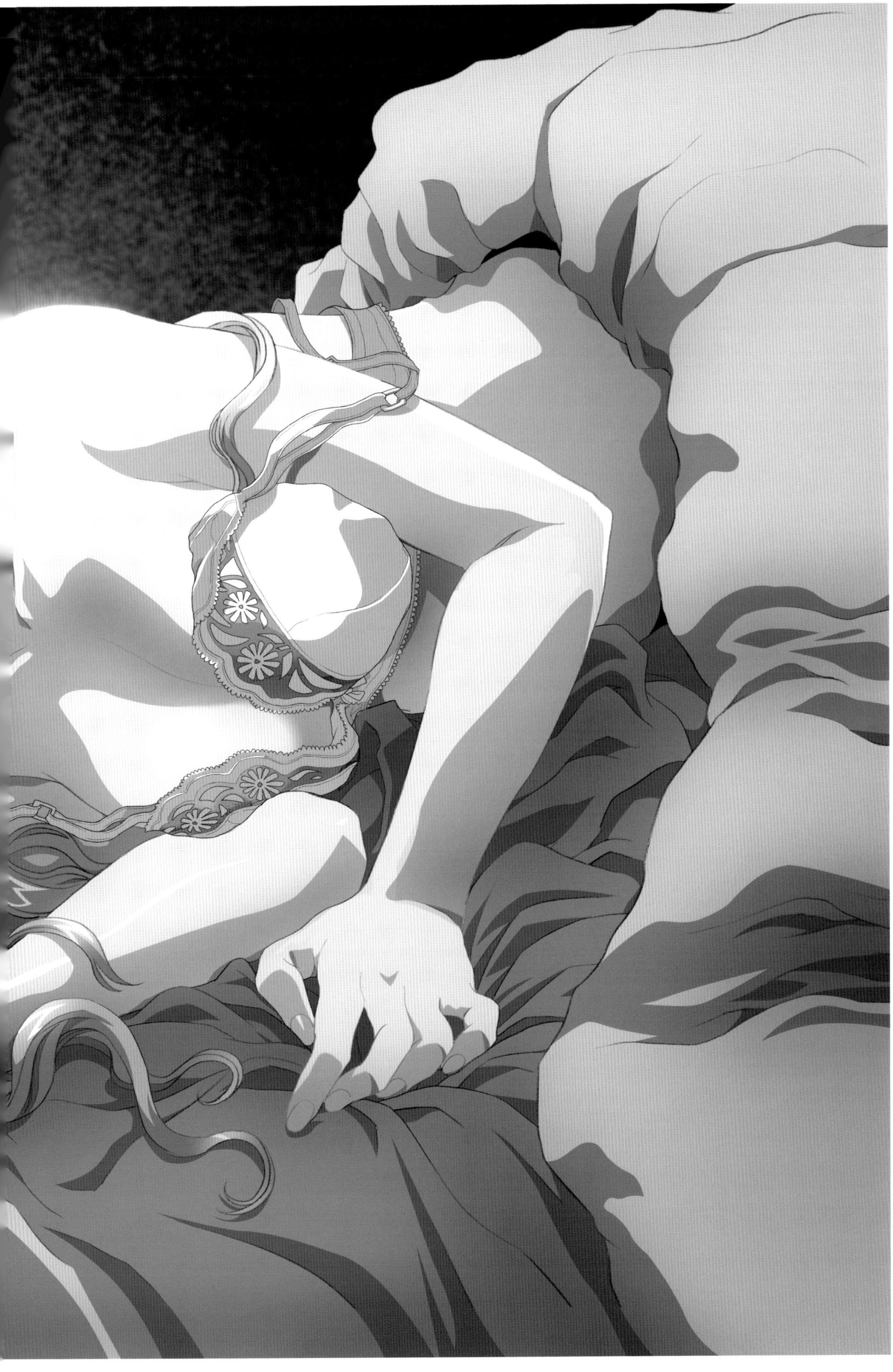

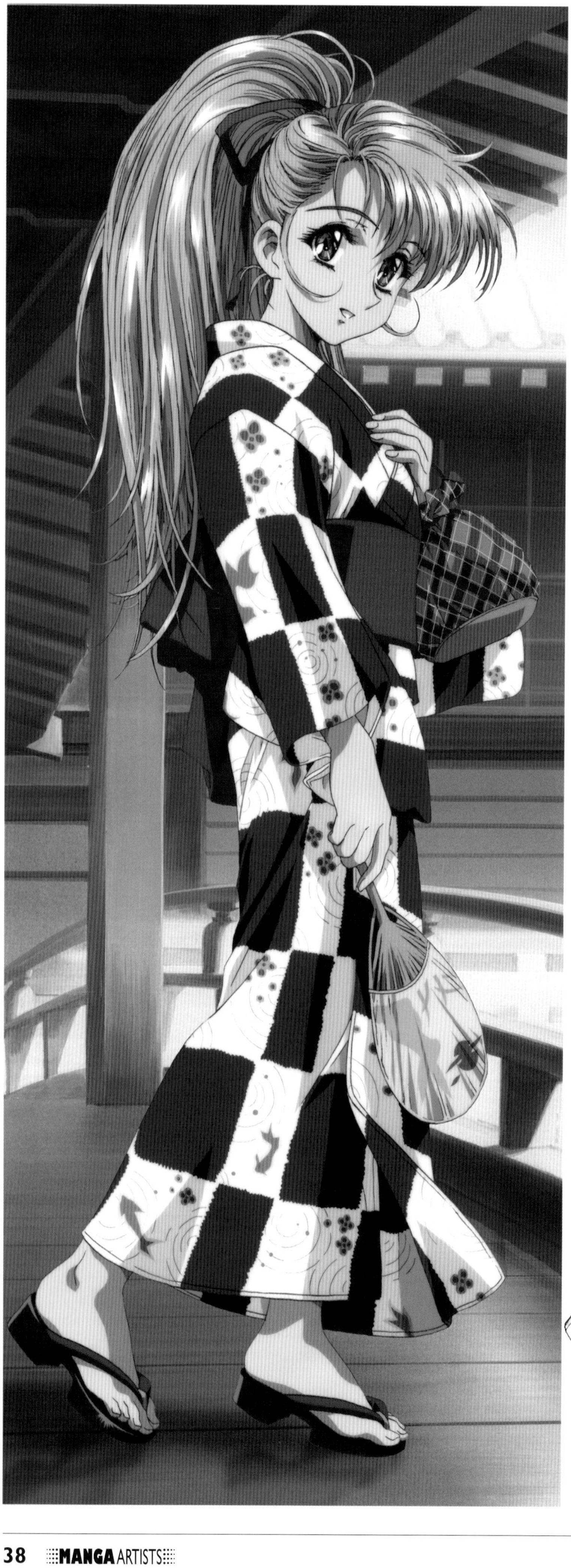

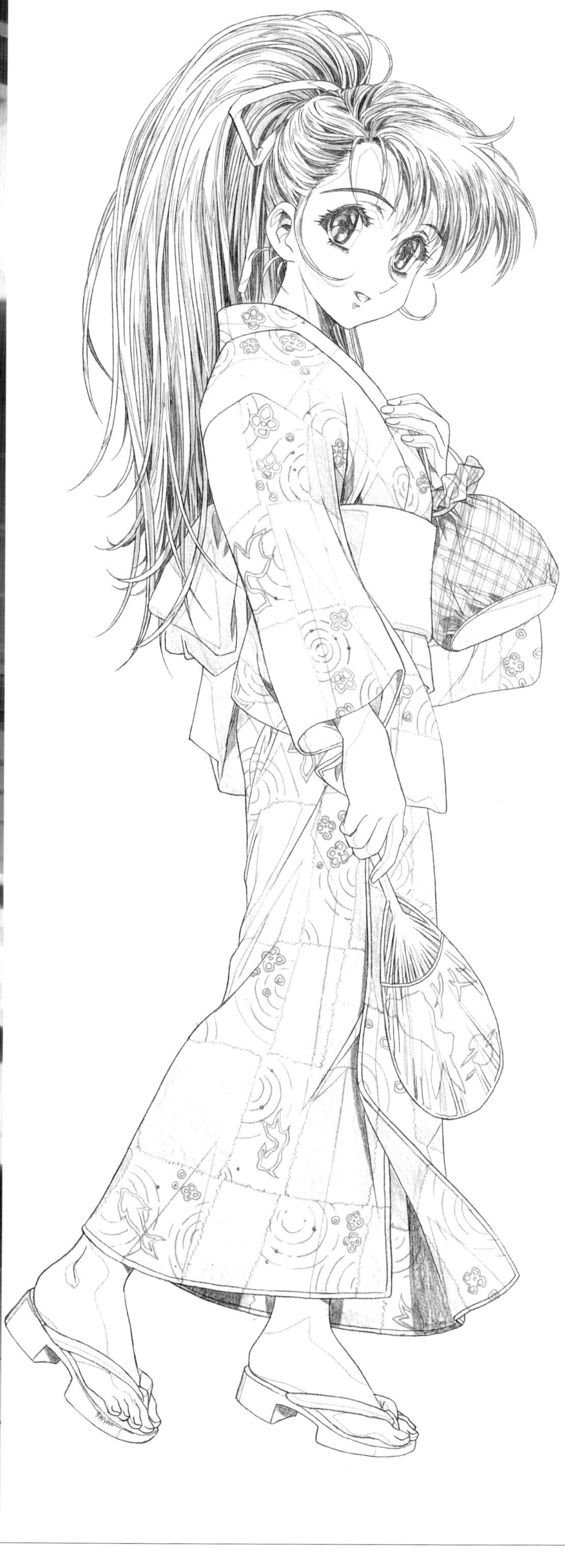

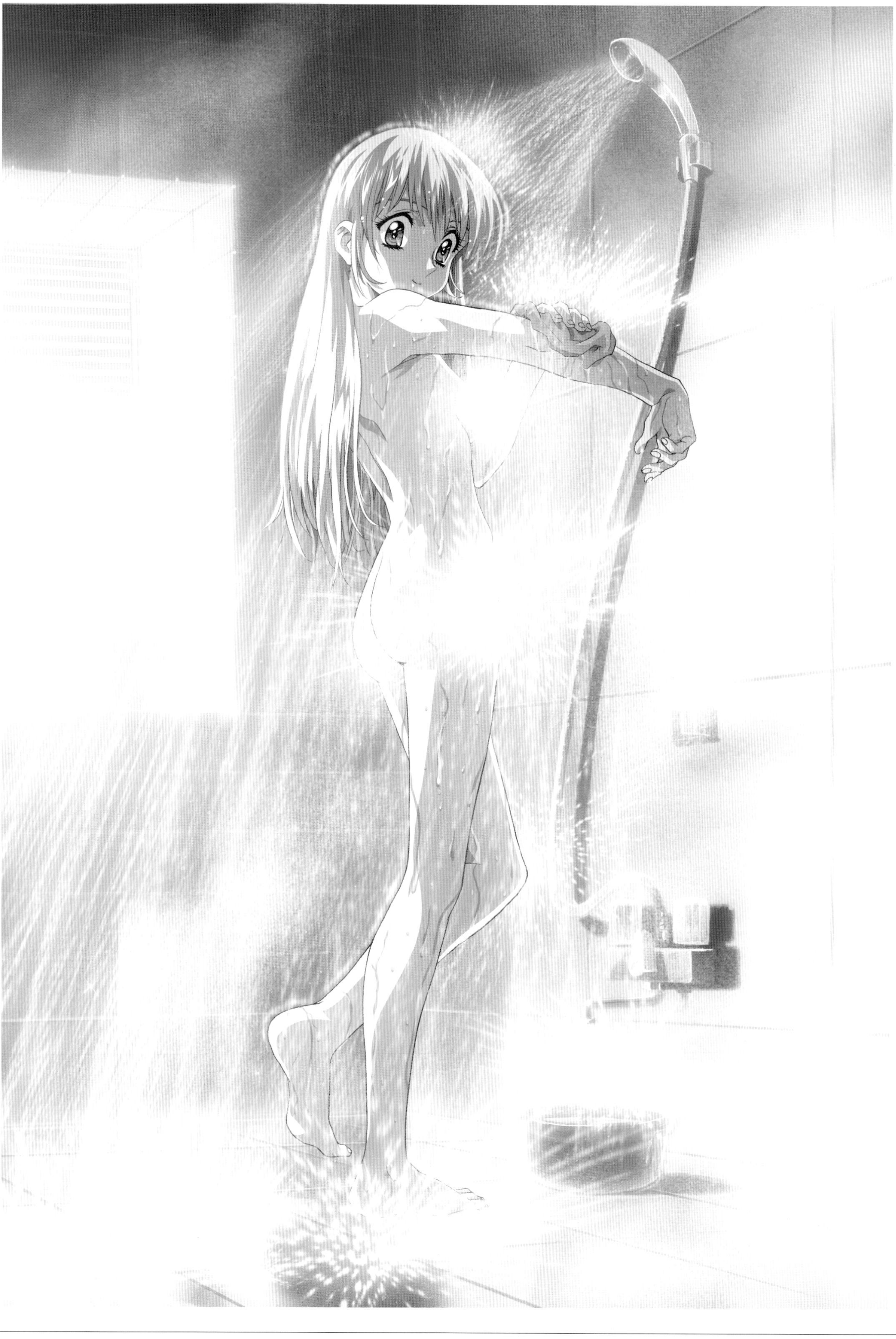

NOUVEIS LOGIC
CLASSIC

Paparazzo on the Dark Side
(Revised edition)

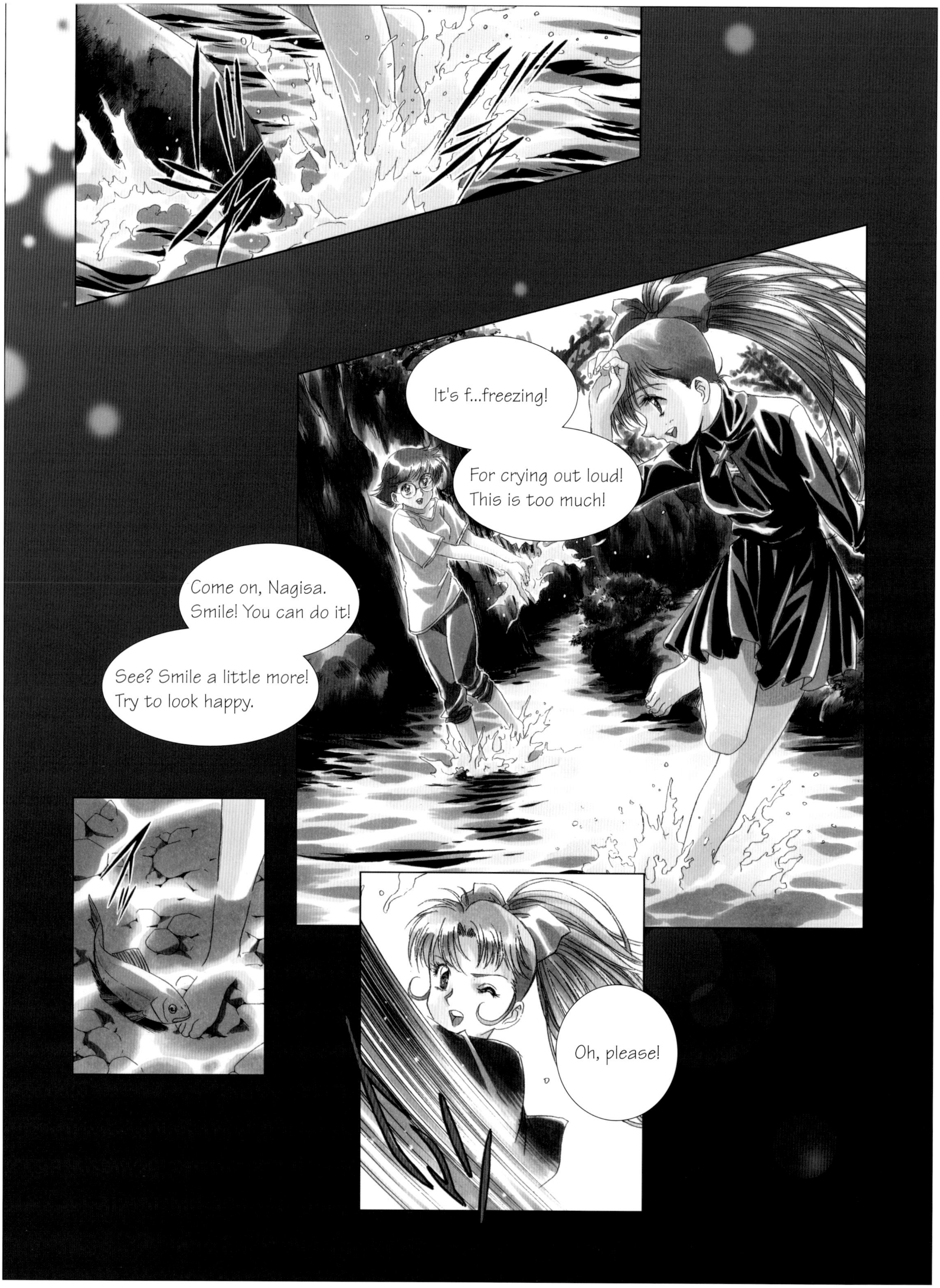
It's f...freezing!
For crying out loud! This is too much!
Come on, Nagisa. Smile! You can do it!
See? Smile a little more! Try to look happy.
Oh, please!

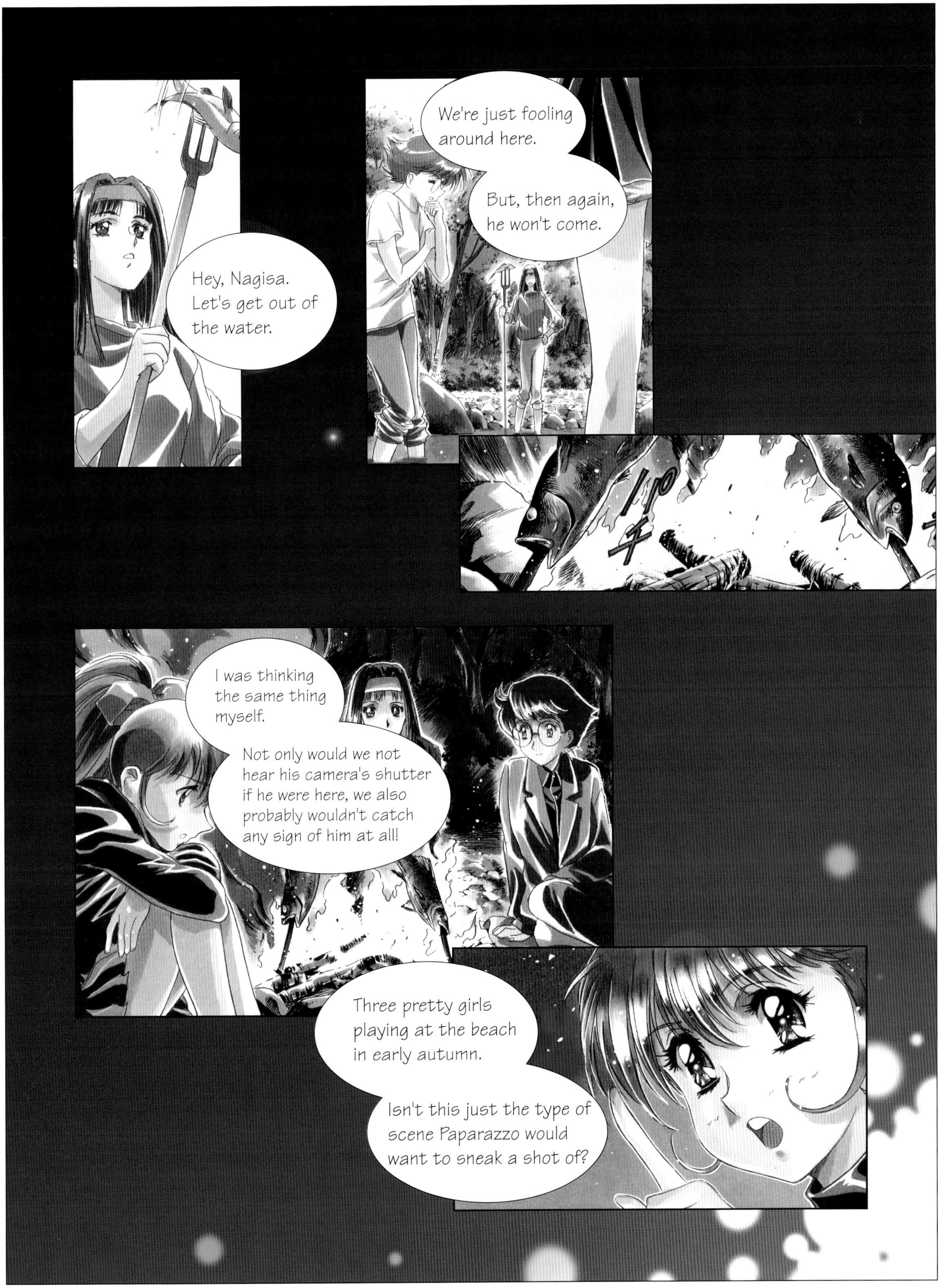
Hey, Nagisa. Let's get out of the water.
We're just fooling around here.
But, then again, he won't come.
I was thinking the same thing myself.
Not only would we not hear his camera's shutter if he were here, we also probably wouldn't catch any sign of him at all!
Three pretty girls playing at the beach in early autumn.
Isn't this just the type of scene Paparazzo would want to sneak a shot of?

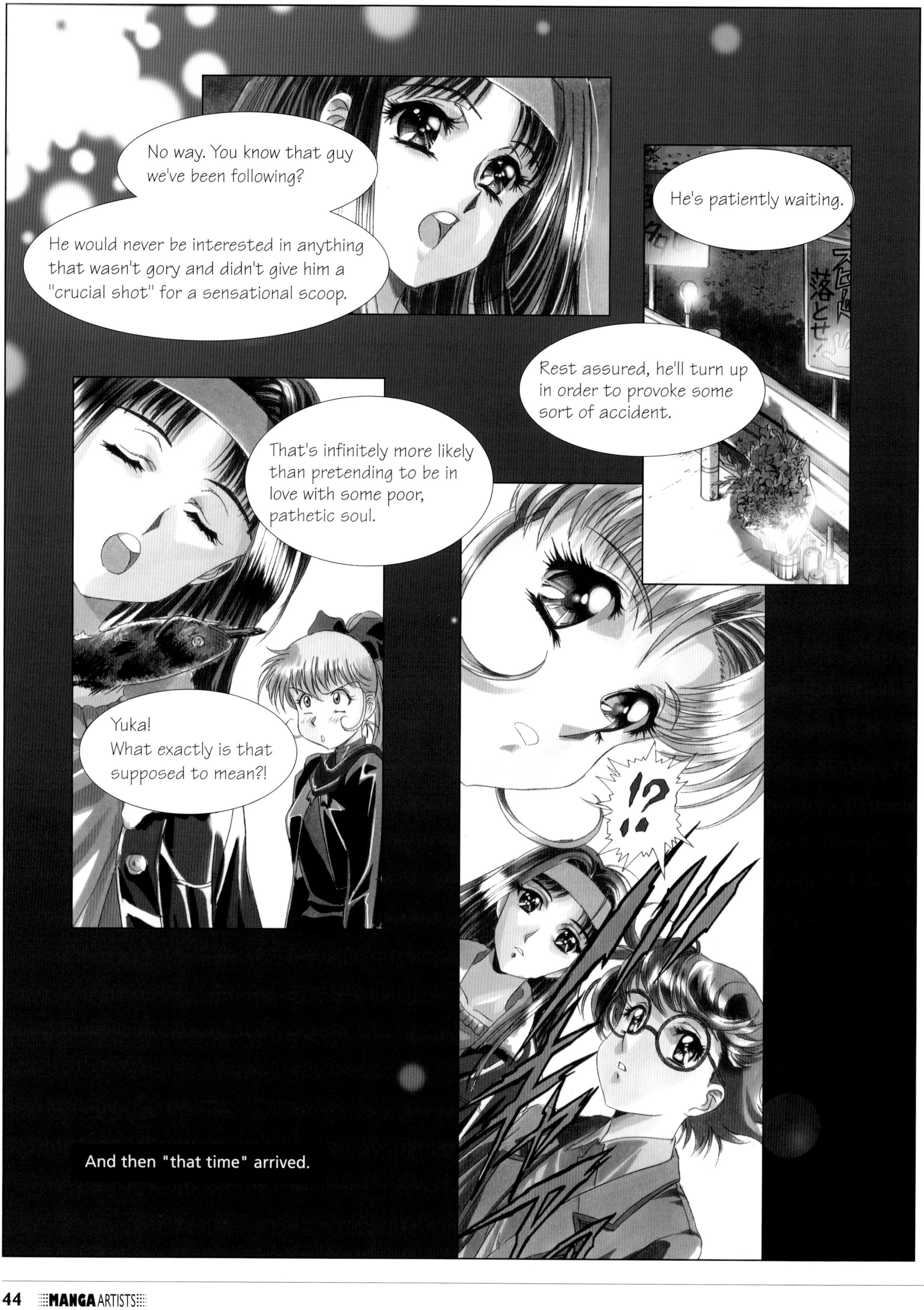
No way. You know that guy we've been following?
He would never be interested in anything that wasn't gory and didn't give him a "crucial shot" for a sensational scoop.
He's patiently waiting.
Rest assured, he'll turn up in order to provoke some sort of accident.
That's infinitely more likely than pretending to be in love with some poor, pathetic soul.
Yuka! What exactly is that supposed to mean?!
!?
And then "that time" arrived.

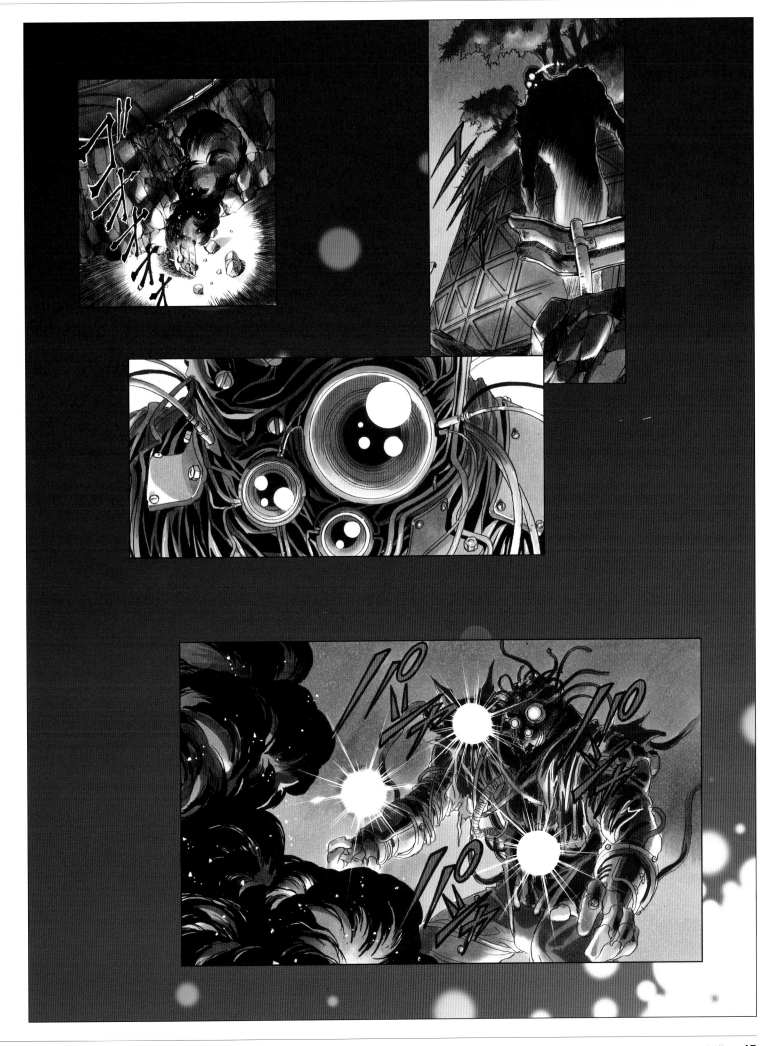

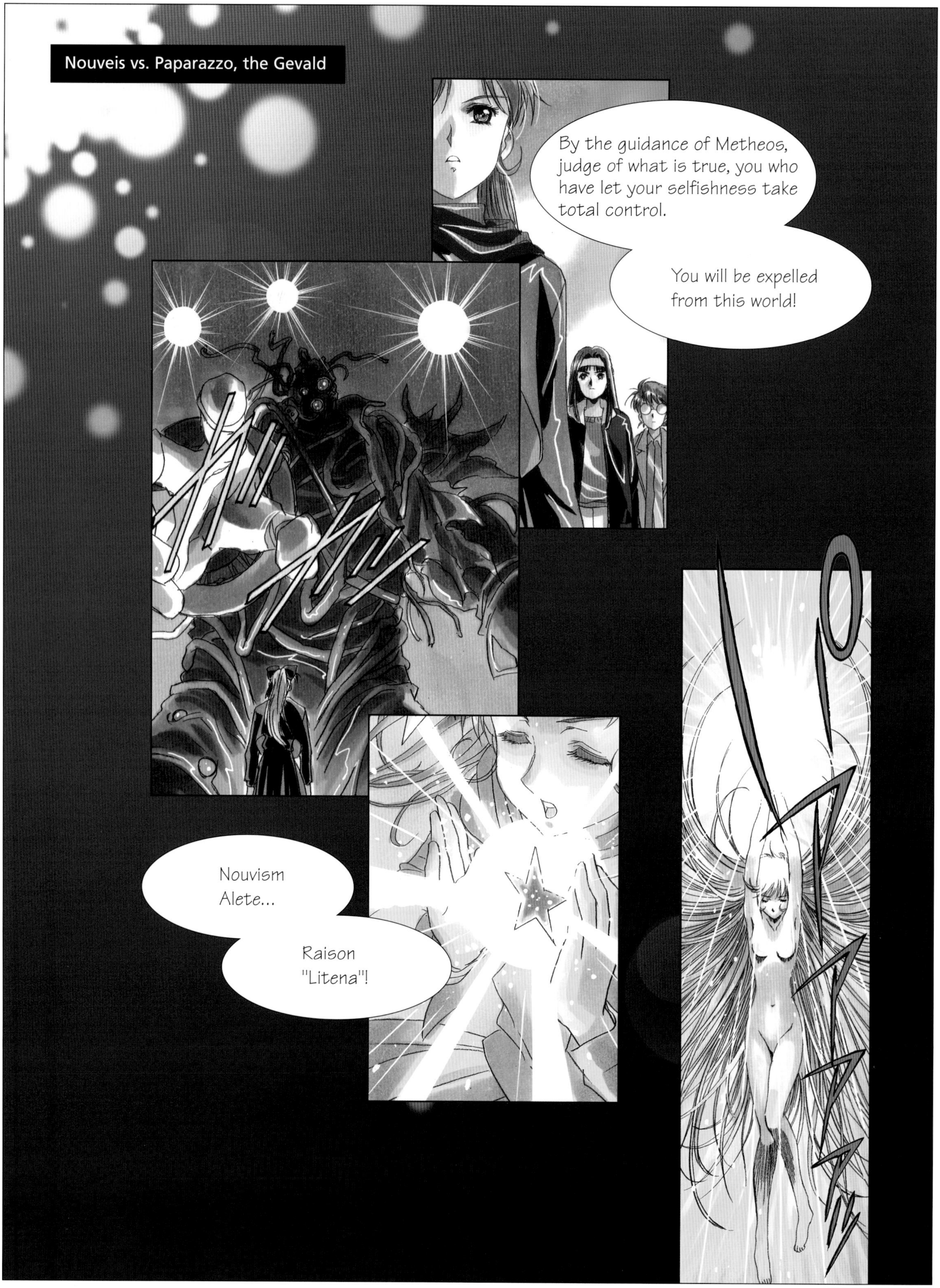
Nouveis vs. Paparazzo, the Gevald
By the guidance of Metheos, judge of what is true, you who have let your selfishness take total control.
You will be expelled from this world!
Nouvism Alete...
Raison "Litena"!

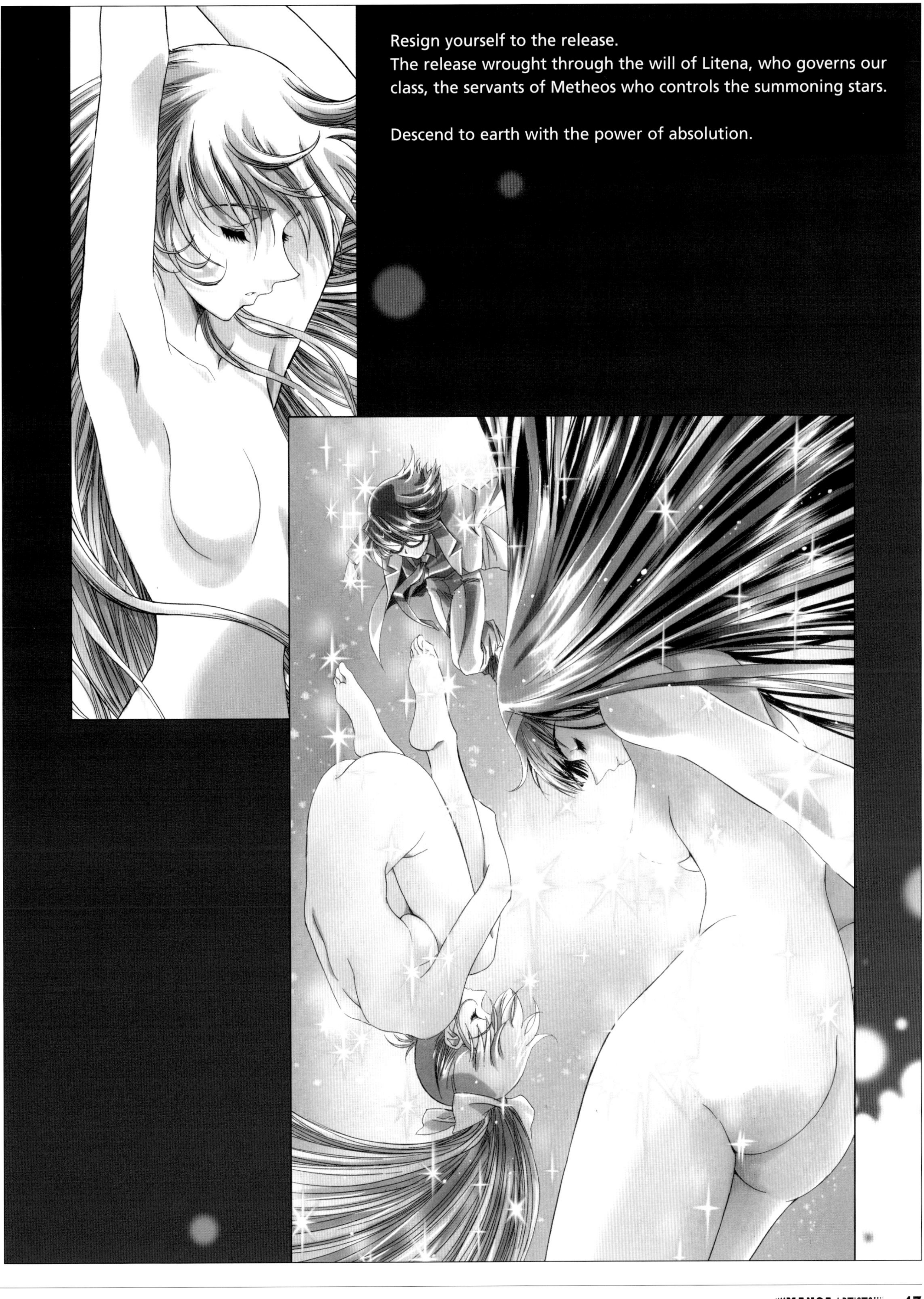
Resign yourself to the release.
The release wrought through the will of Litena, who governs our class, the servants of Metheos who controls the summoning stars.
Descend to earth with the power of absolution.

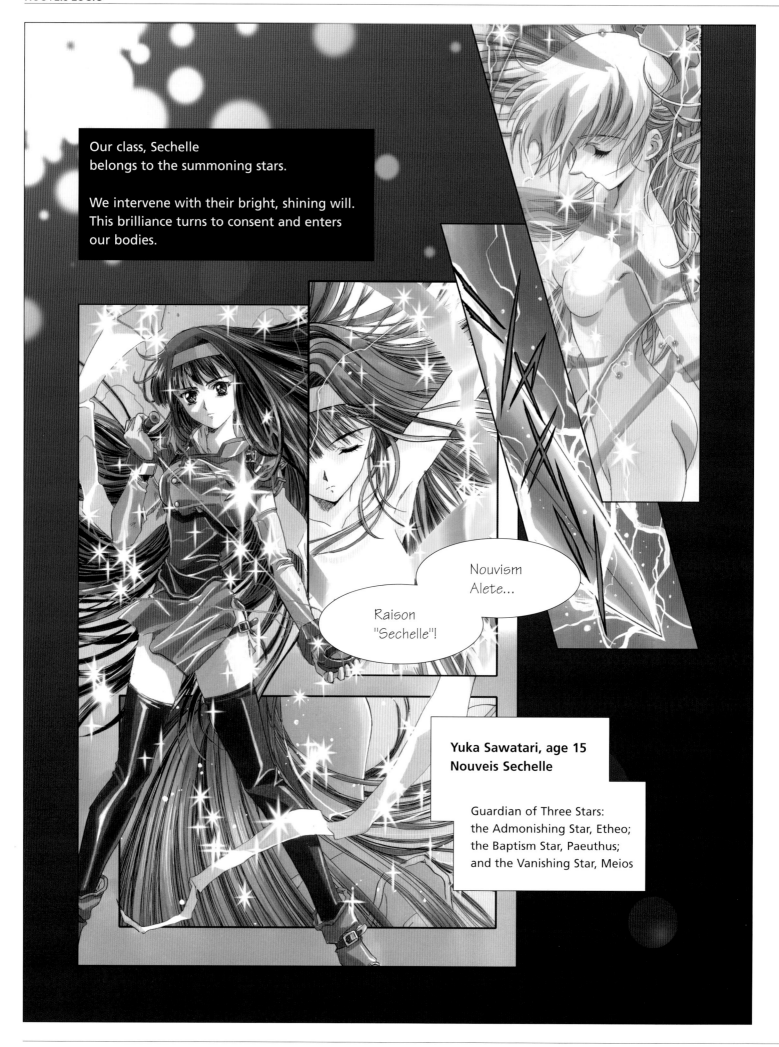

Our class, Sechelle
belongs to the summoning stars.

We intervene with their bright, shining will.
This brilliance turns to consent and enters
our bodies.

Nouvism
Alete...

Raison
"Sechelle"!

**Yuka Sawatari, age 15
Nouveis Sechelle**

Guardian of Three Stars:
the Admonishing Star, Etheo;
the Baptism Star, Paeuthus;
and the Vanishing Star, Meios

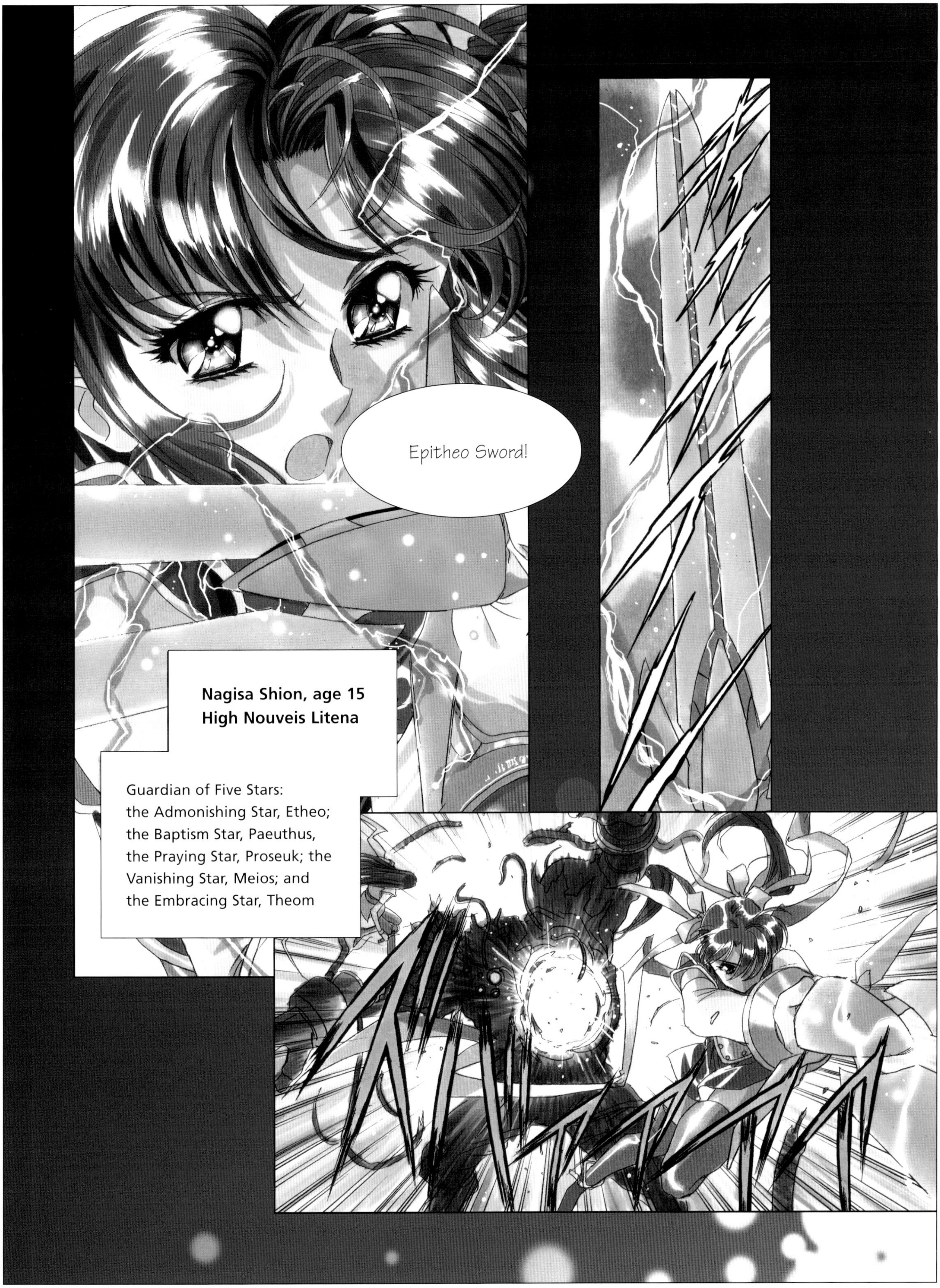
Epitheo Sword!
Nagisa Shion, age 15
High Nouveis Litena
Guardian of Five Stars: the Admonishing Star, Etheo; the Baptism Star, Paeuthus, the Praying Star, Proseuk; the Vanishing Star, Meios; and the Embracing Star, Theom

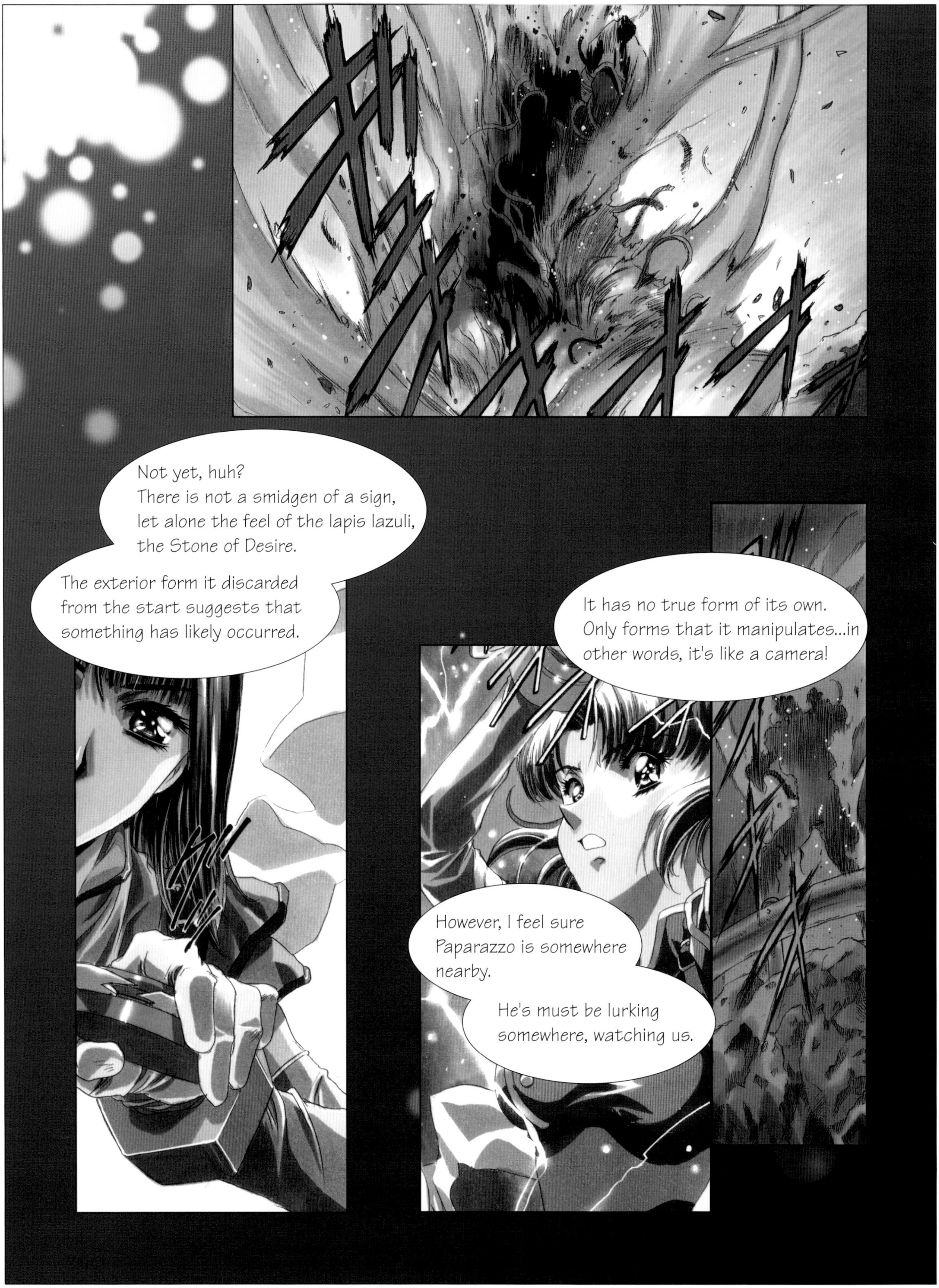
It has no true form of its own.
Only forms that it manipulates...in other words, it's like a camera!
Not yet, huh?
There is not a smidgen of a sign, let alone the feel of the lapis lazuli, the Stone of Desire.
The exterior form it discarded from the start suggests that something has likely occurred.
However, I feel sure Paparazzo is somewhere nearby.
He's must be lurking somewhere, watching us.

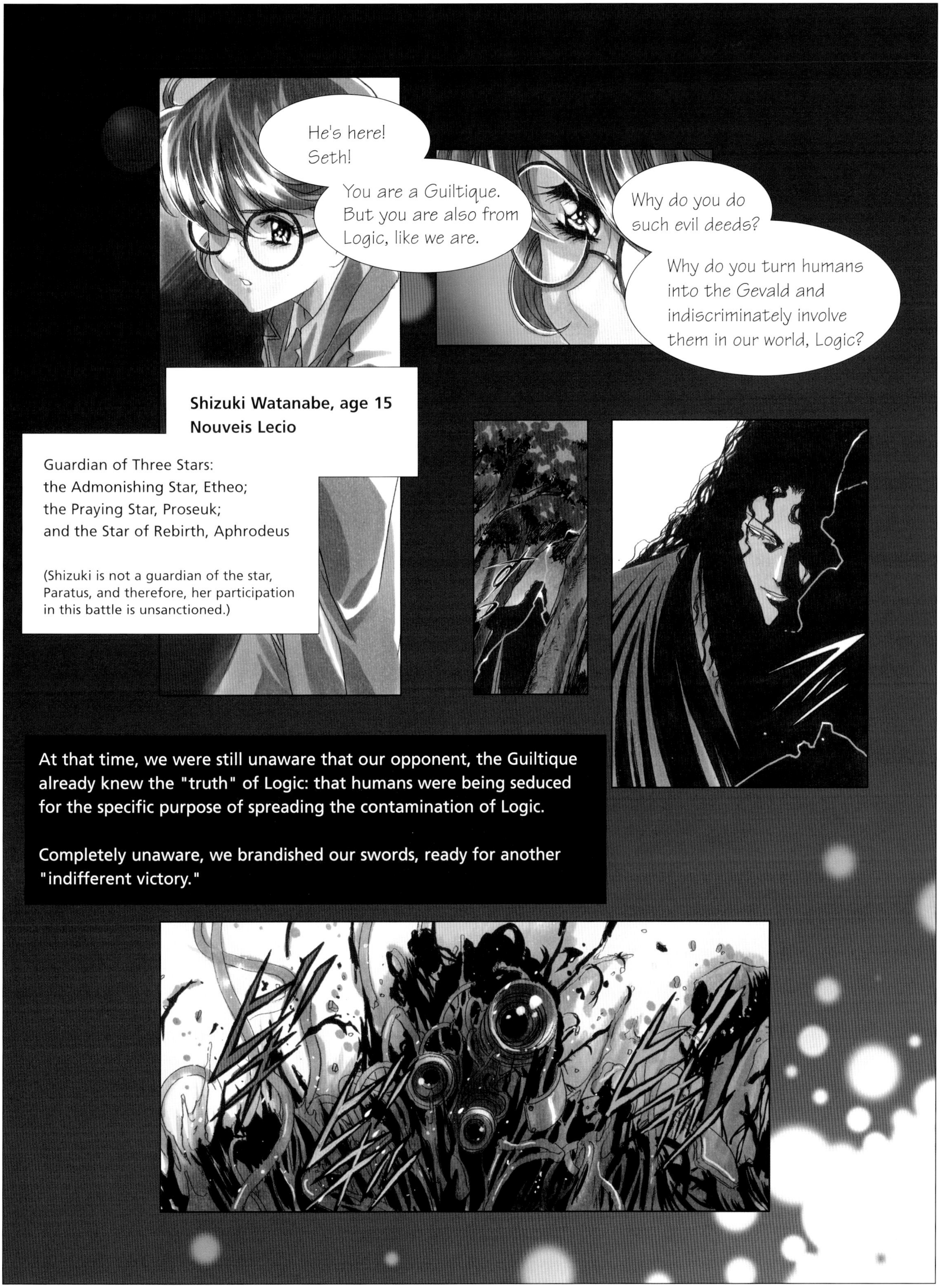
He's here! Seth!
You are a Guiltique. But you are also from Logic, like we are.
Why do you do such evil deeds?
Why do you turn humans into the Gevald and indiscriminately involve them in our world, Logic?
Shizuki Watanabe, age 15
Nouveis Lecio
Guardian of Three Stars: the Admonishing Star, Etheo; the Praying Star, Proseuk; and the Star of Rebirth, Aphrodeus
(Shizuki is not a guardian of the star, Paratus, and therefore, her participation in this battle is unsanctioned.)
At that time, we were still unaware that our opponent, the Guiltique already knew the "truth" of Logic: that humans were being seduced for the specific purpose of spreading the contamination of Logic.
Completely unaware, we brandished our swords, ready for another "indifferent victory."

Nouveis Logic
Paparazzo in the Dark Side
(Published 1997 to 1999)

These excerpts were originally produced in 1997 and
released as Parts I and II. These excerpts have been
restructured to fit this publication.

KOH KAWARAJIMA

Illustration Collection
Author's Selection

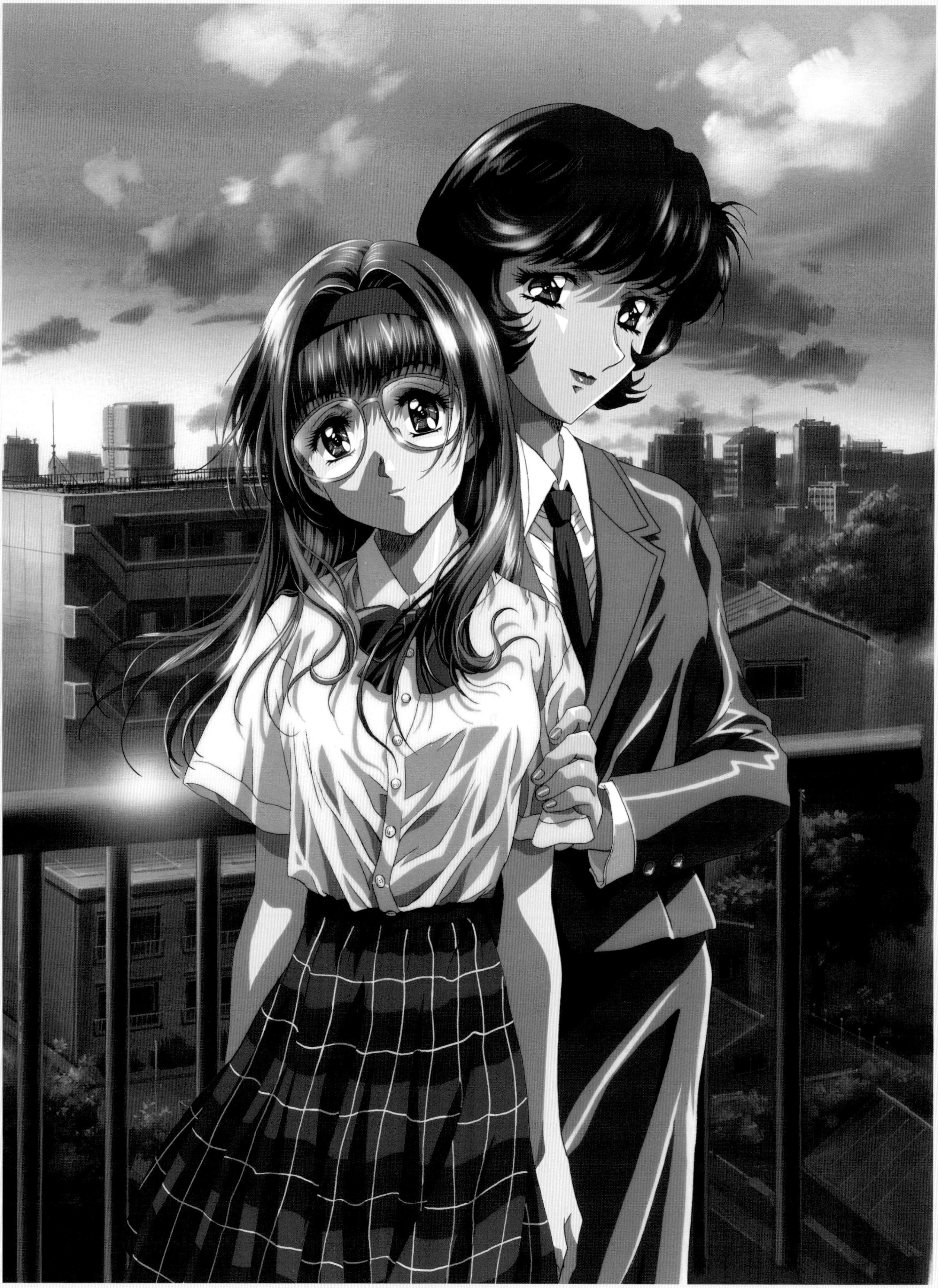

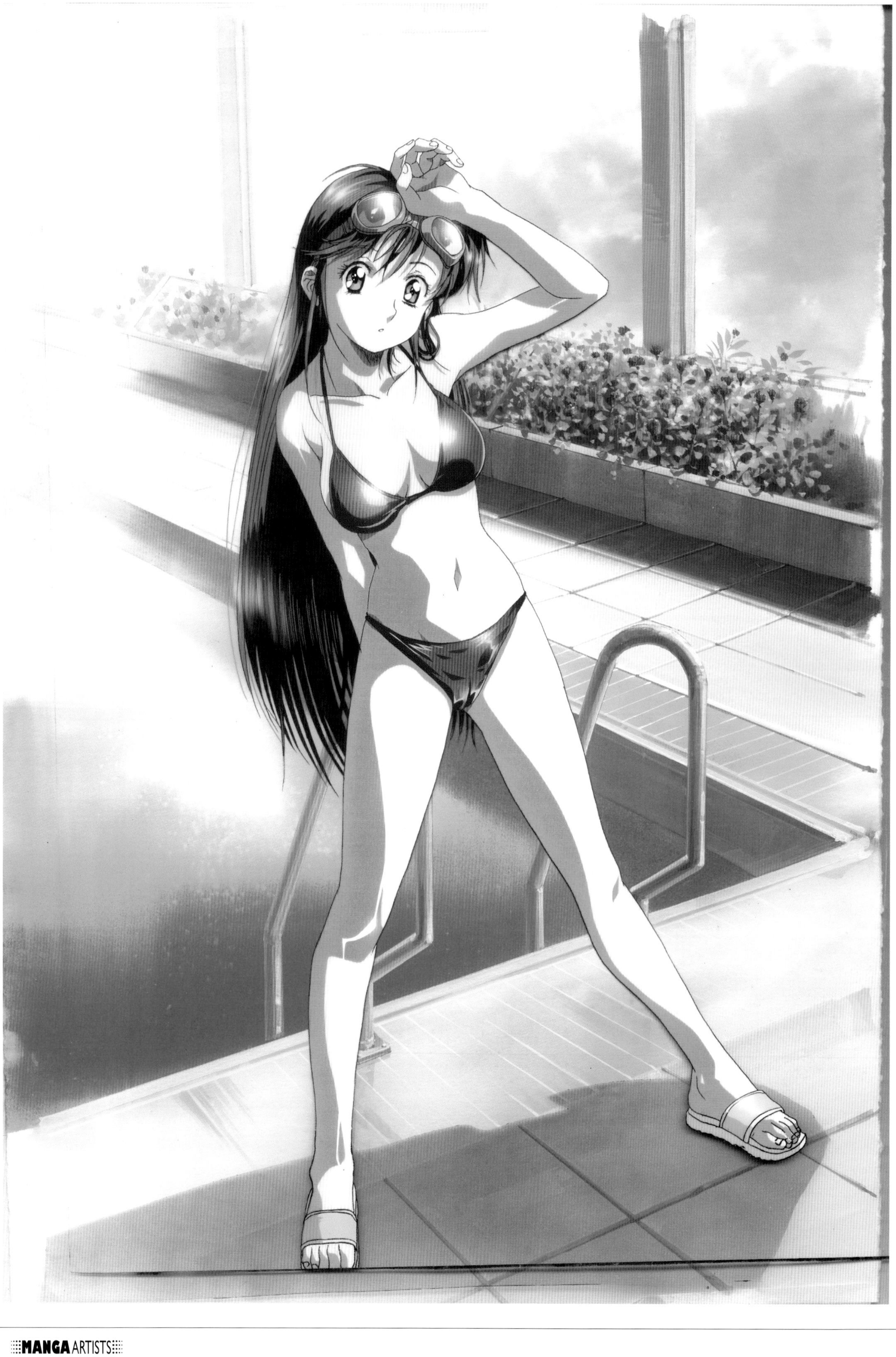

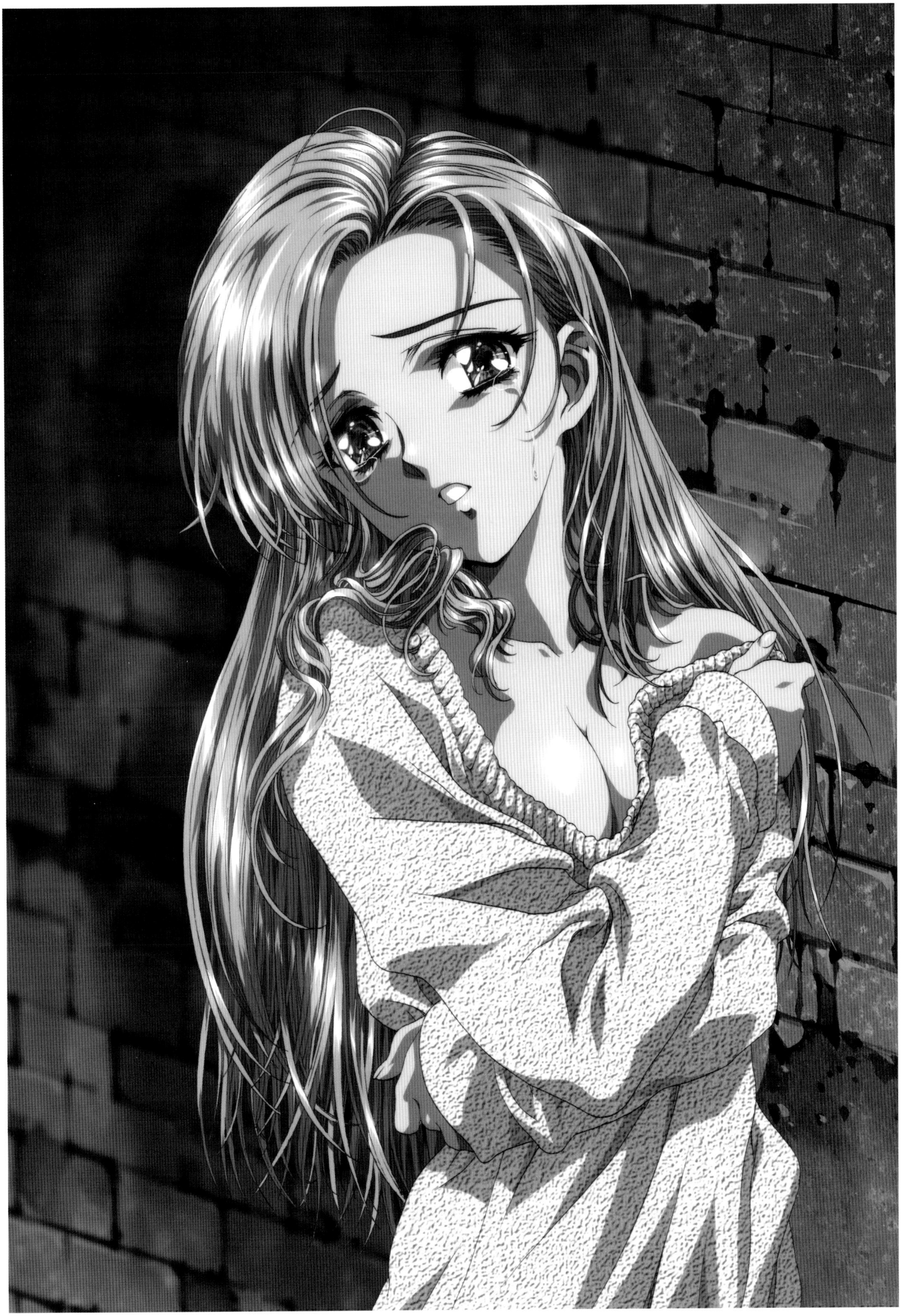

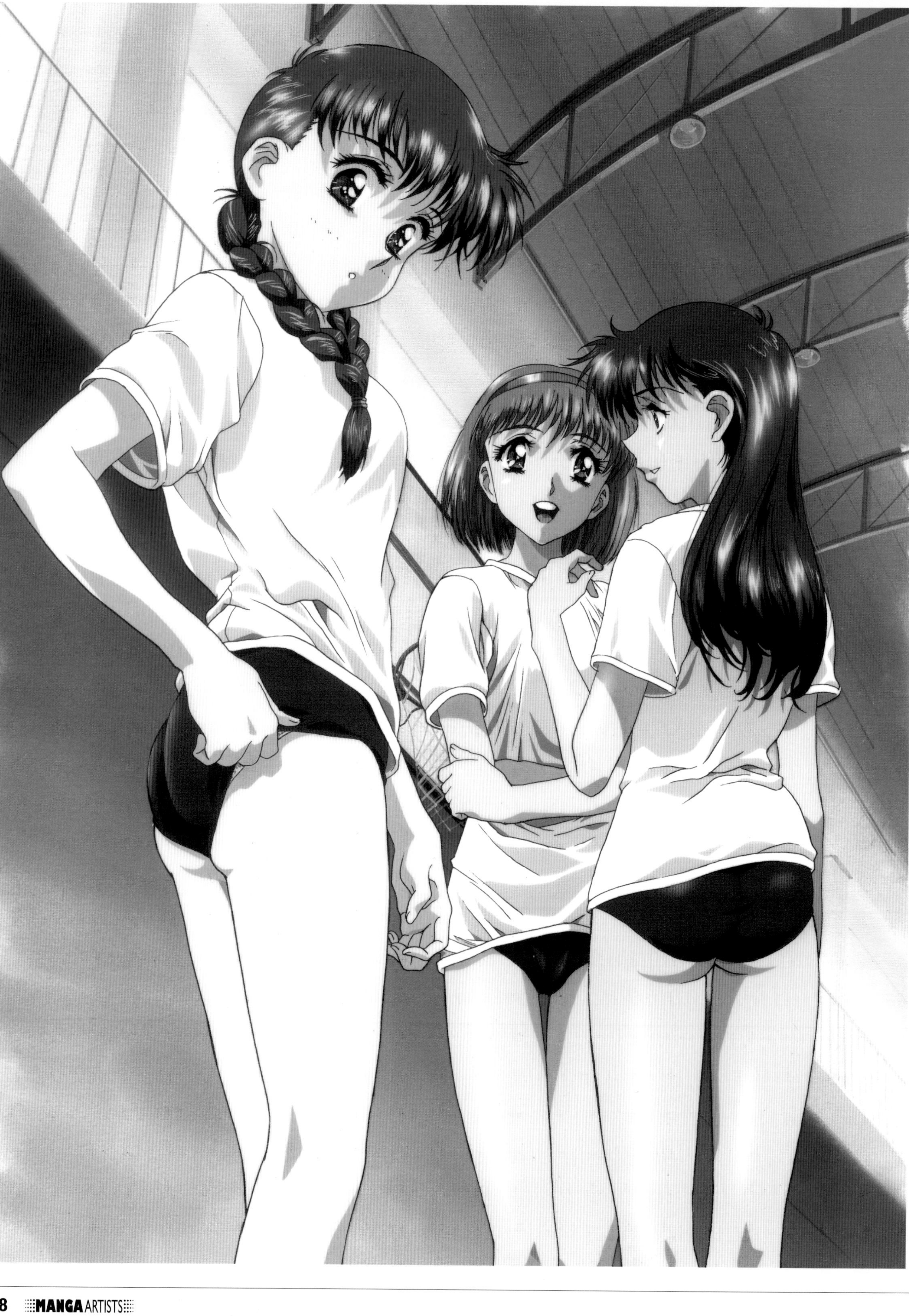

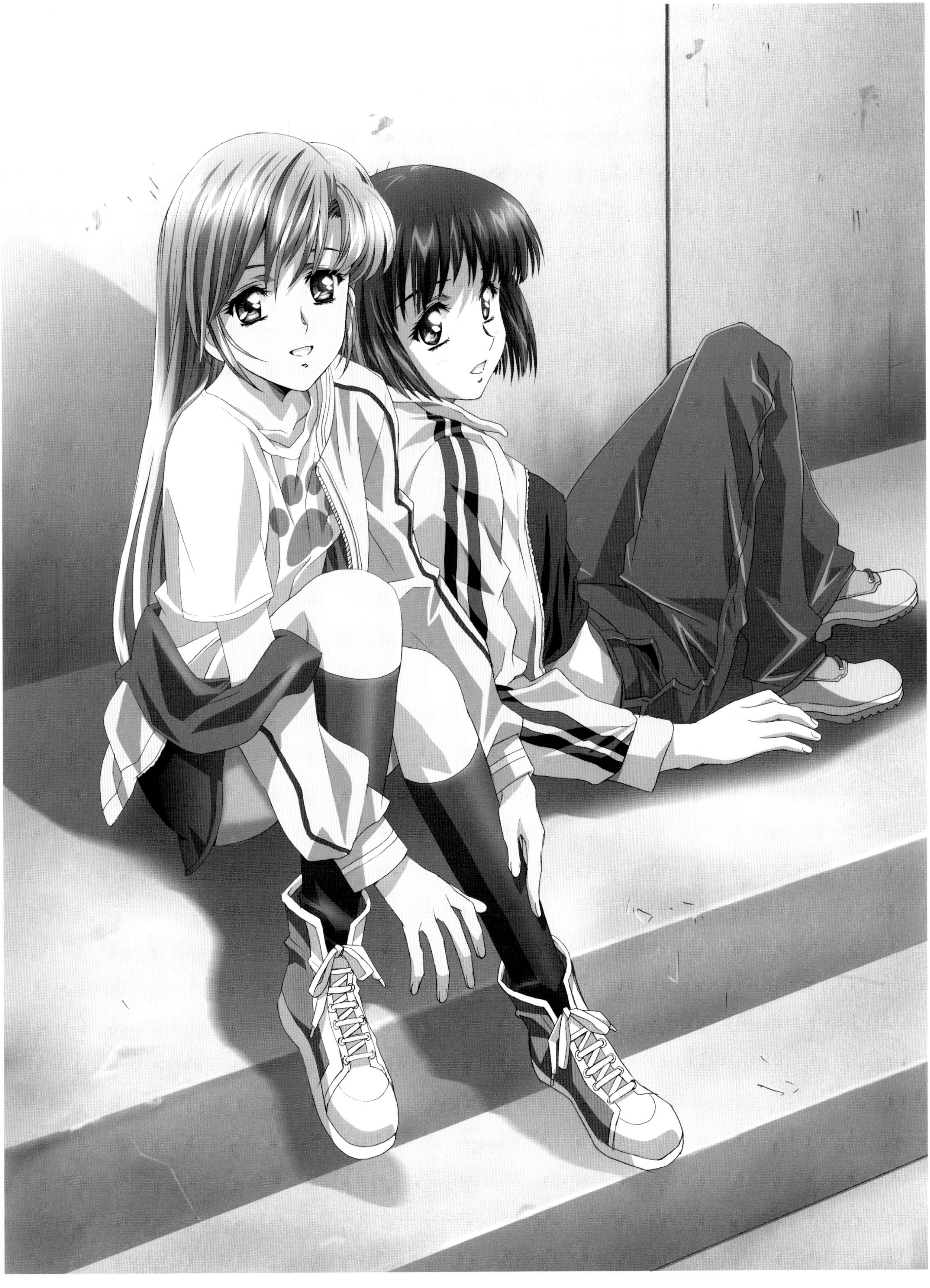

The Artist's Sketchbook

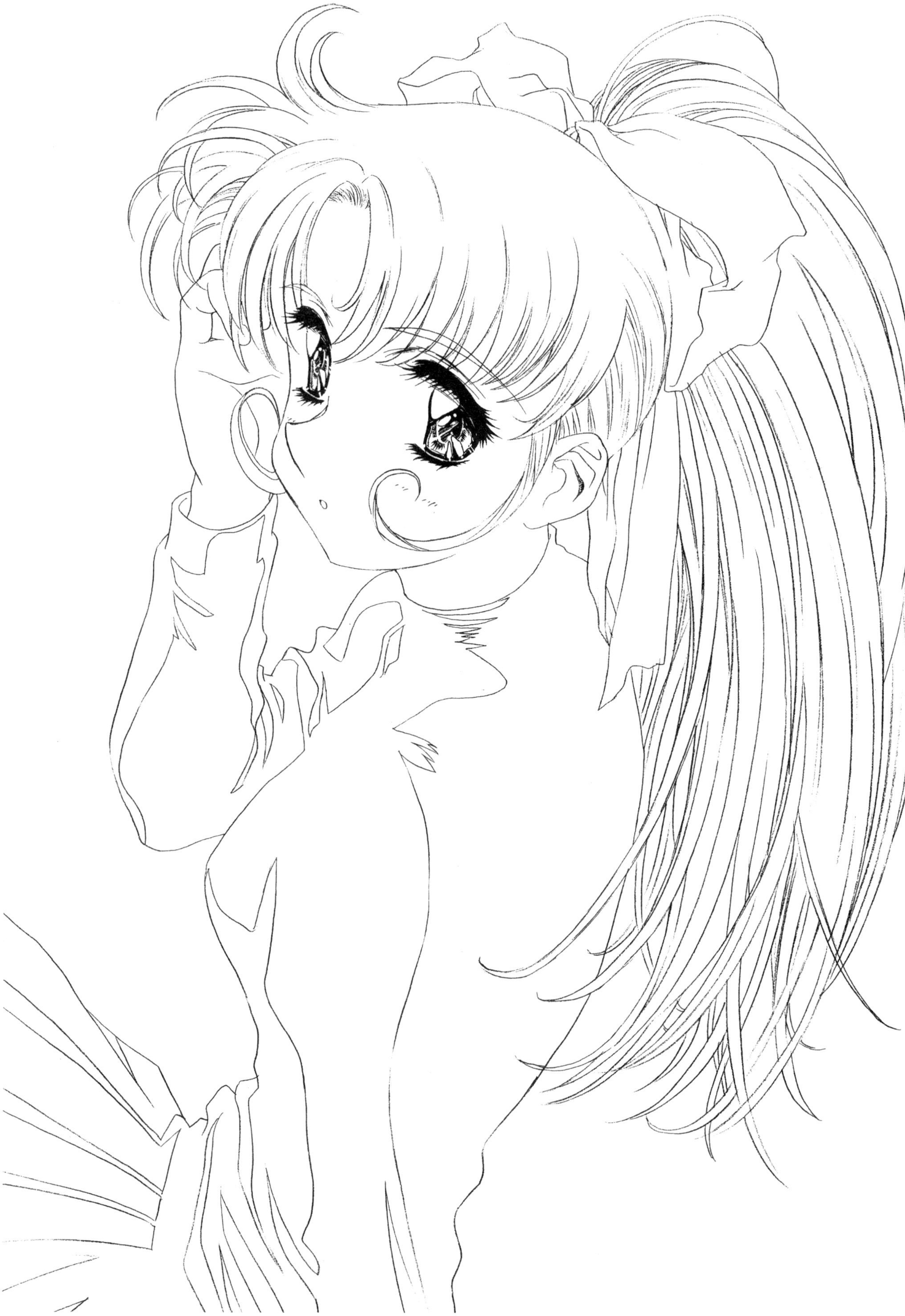

Illustration Production the Kawarajima Way

Key Points

Synthetic and Mechanical Objects

First, I try to capture the overall form, adding the details later. No matter how detailed the drawing, if the composition is not satisfactory, then all I've done is produced an extravagant lump. Therefore, I take extreme care with this point.

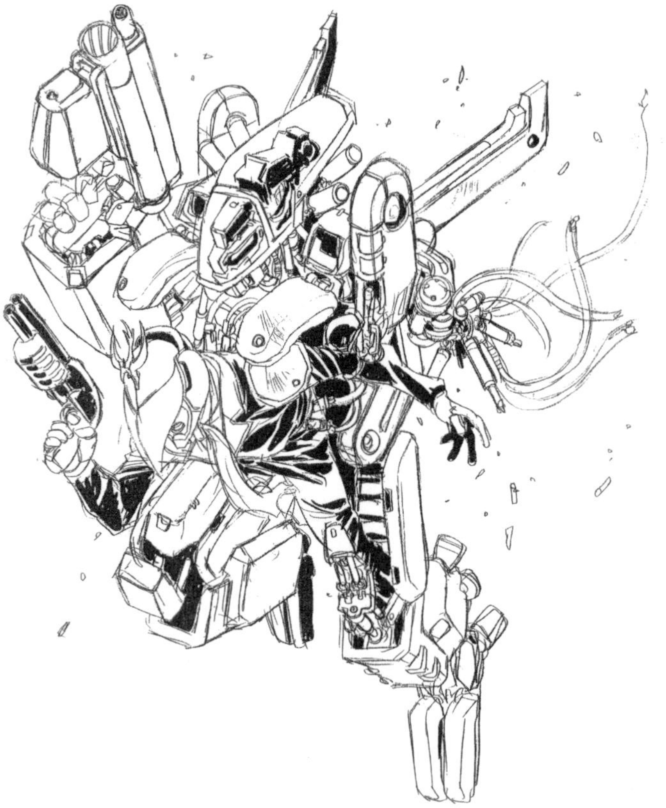

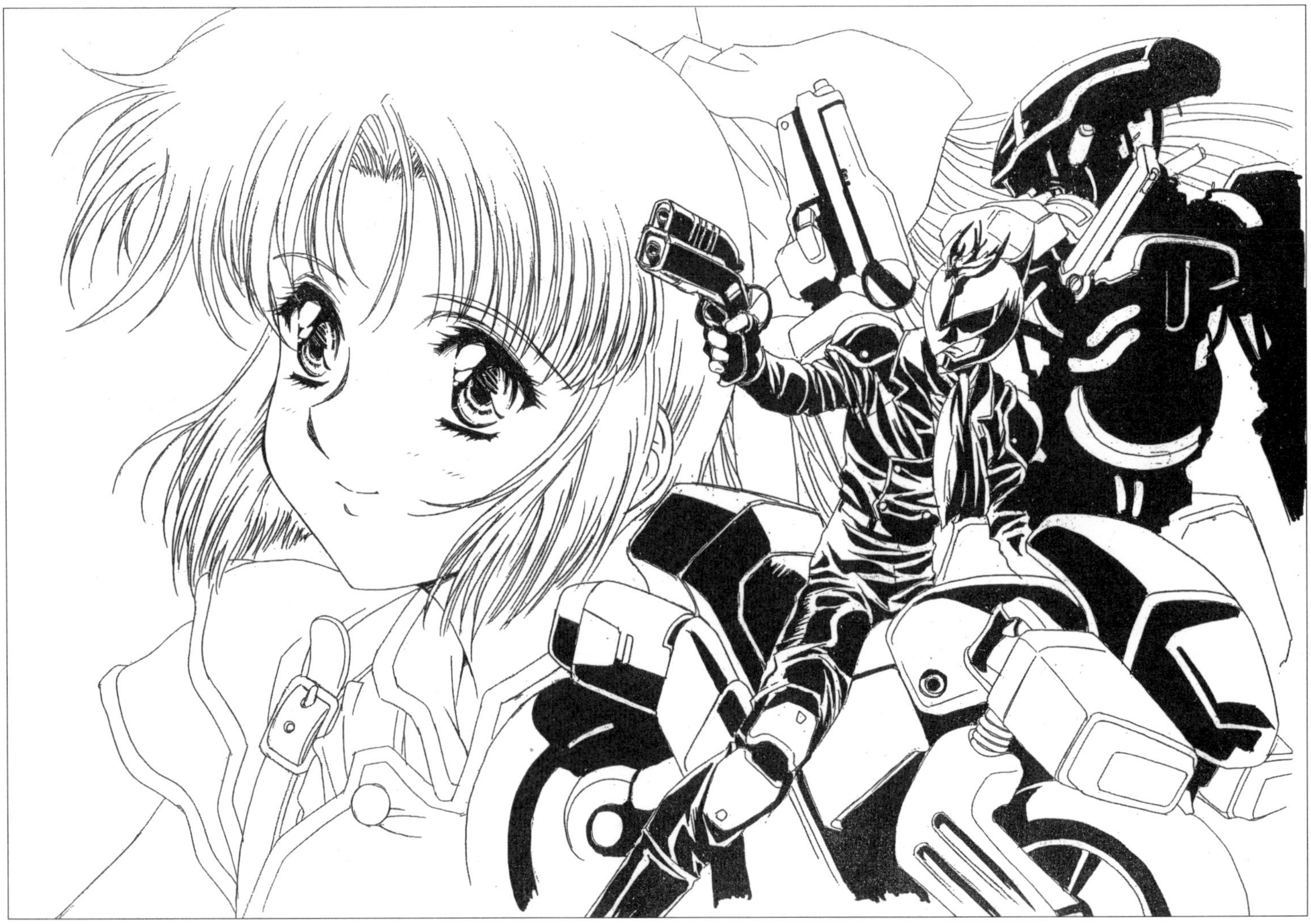

This is an illustration I did before the actual beginning of the story, so the atmosphere projected by this composition is a bit different from what I'm drawing now.

Illustration Production the Kawarajima Way

Key Points

Costumes

I drew this illustration after receiving a request to create a design model for a [plastic] figure to be produced. My costume concept was to imbue it with a traditional "Japanese" kimono sensibility. Consequently, if you compare it to a purely "fantasy world" type of costume, it may come across as a bit unorthodox.

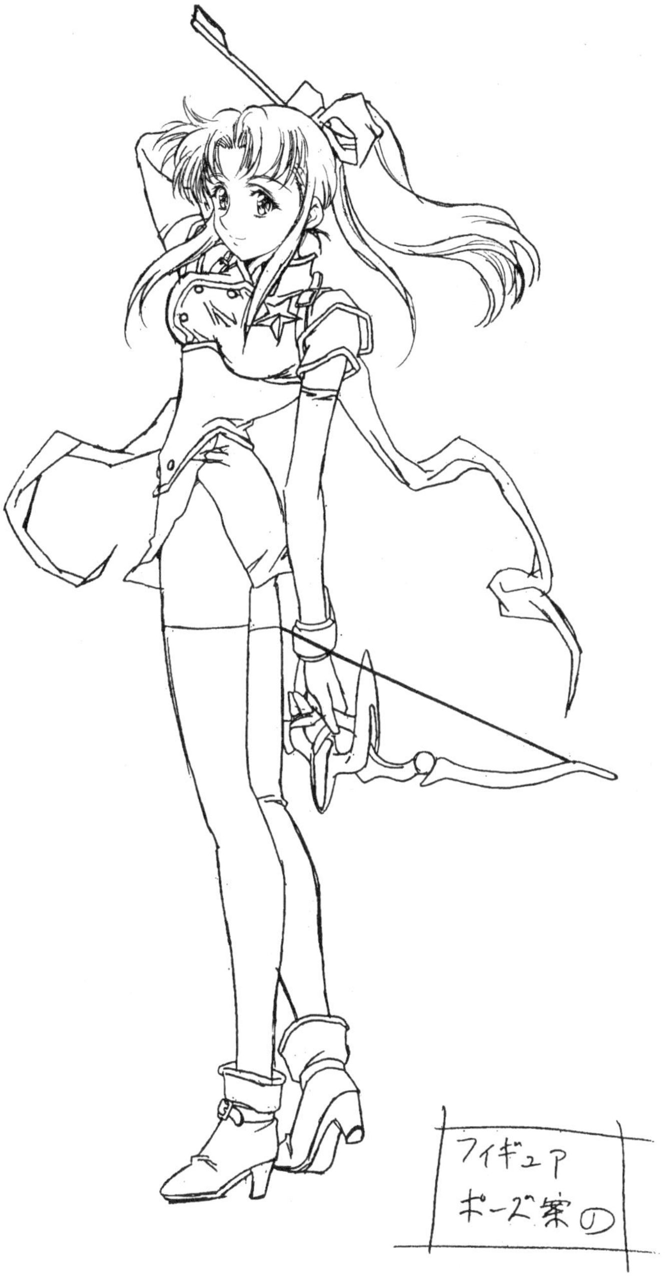
フィギュア
ポーズ案①

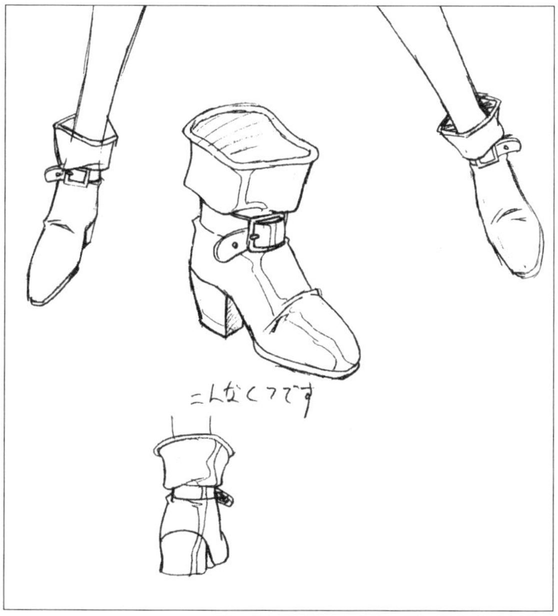
こんなくつです

The figure prototype artist asked me to provide more detail for the boots, so I added them later.

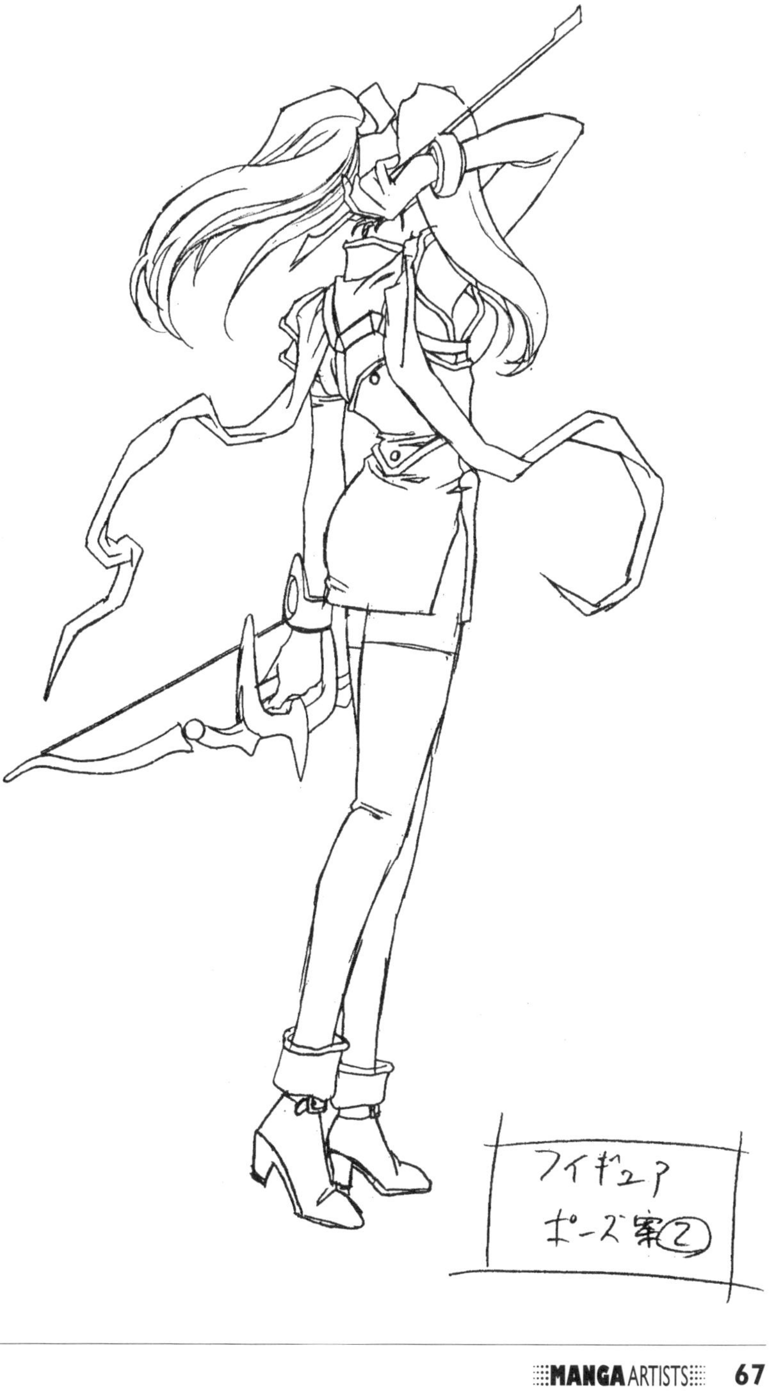
フィギュア
ポーズ案②

Illustration Production the Kawarajima Way

Key Points

Image

In order to impart my artwork a sense of vibrancy and of actually being there, I make efforts to study and observe those around me constantly and on a daily basis. I am always considering how I can effectively reflect in my artwork visual knowledge I have gained of things' actual state. In my project *Nouveis Logic*, I eagerly incorporated the present into my artwork while wishing to expand the scope of expression in which I was proficient, even by just a bit.

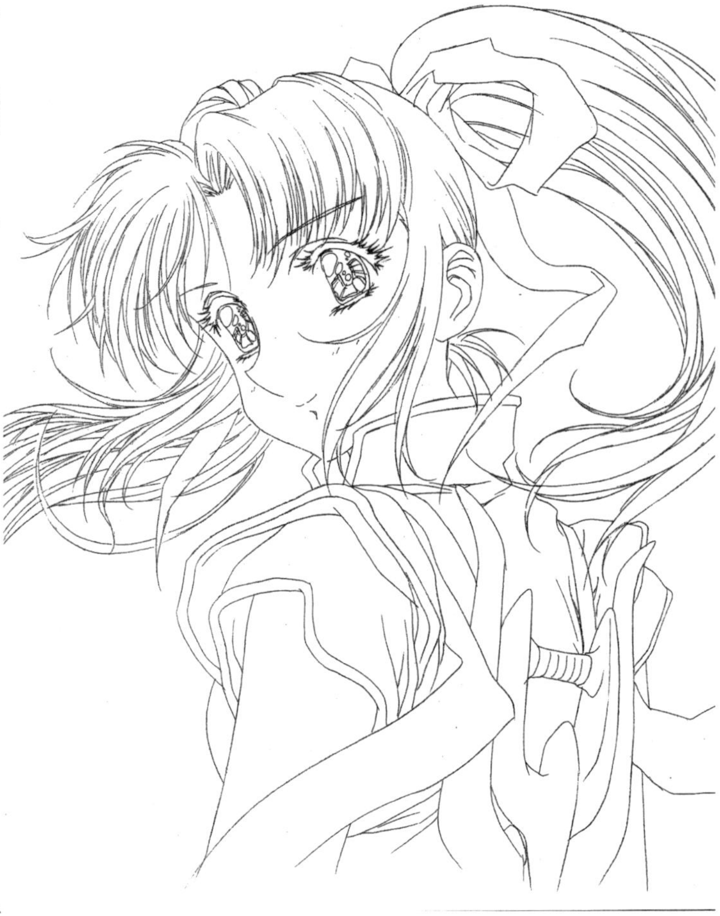

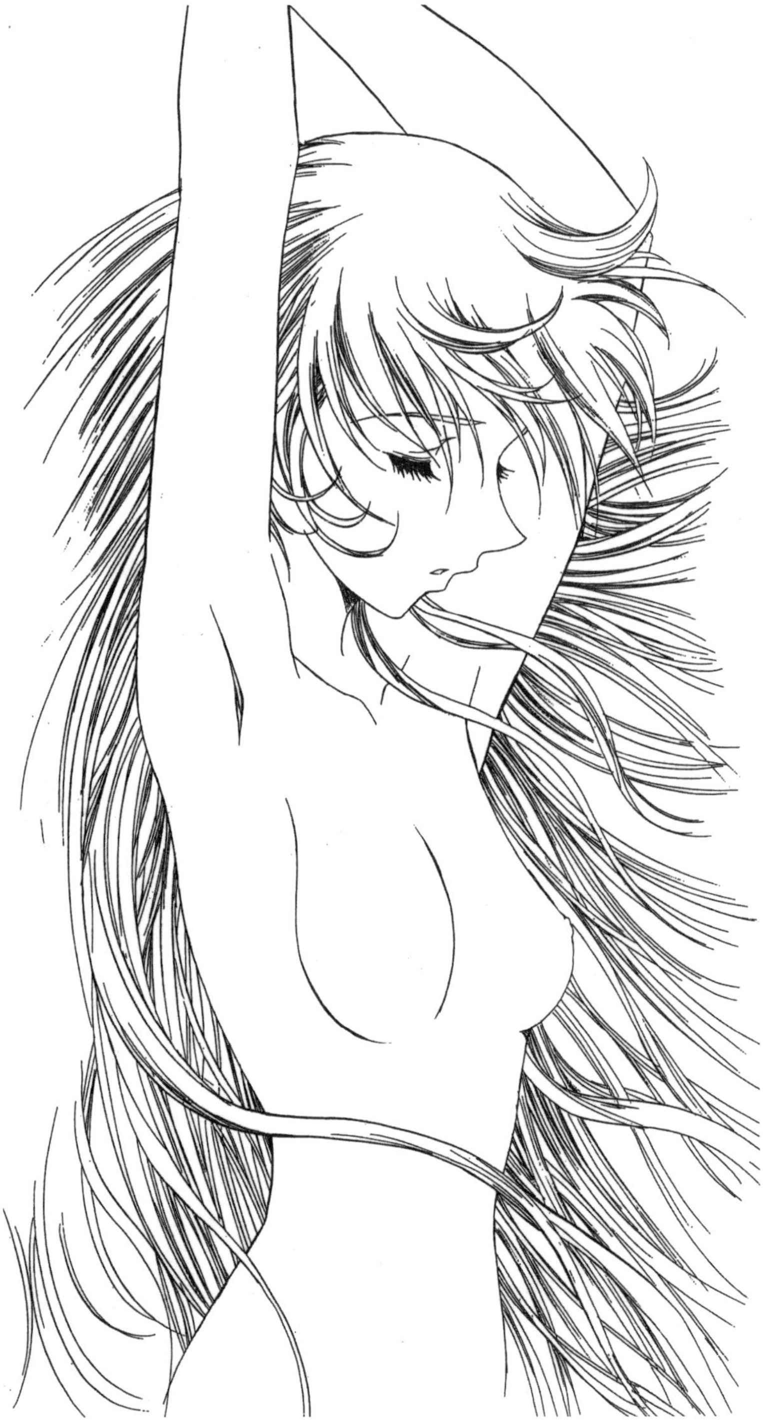

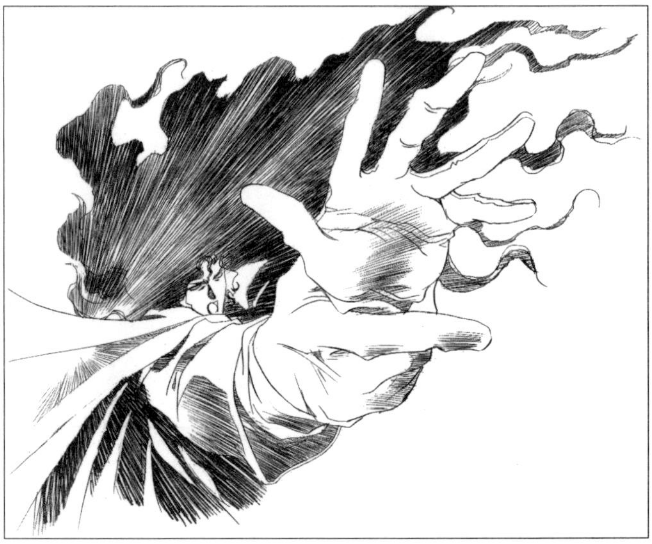

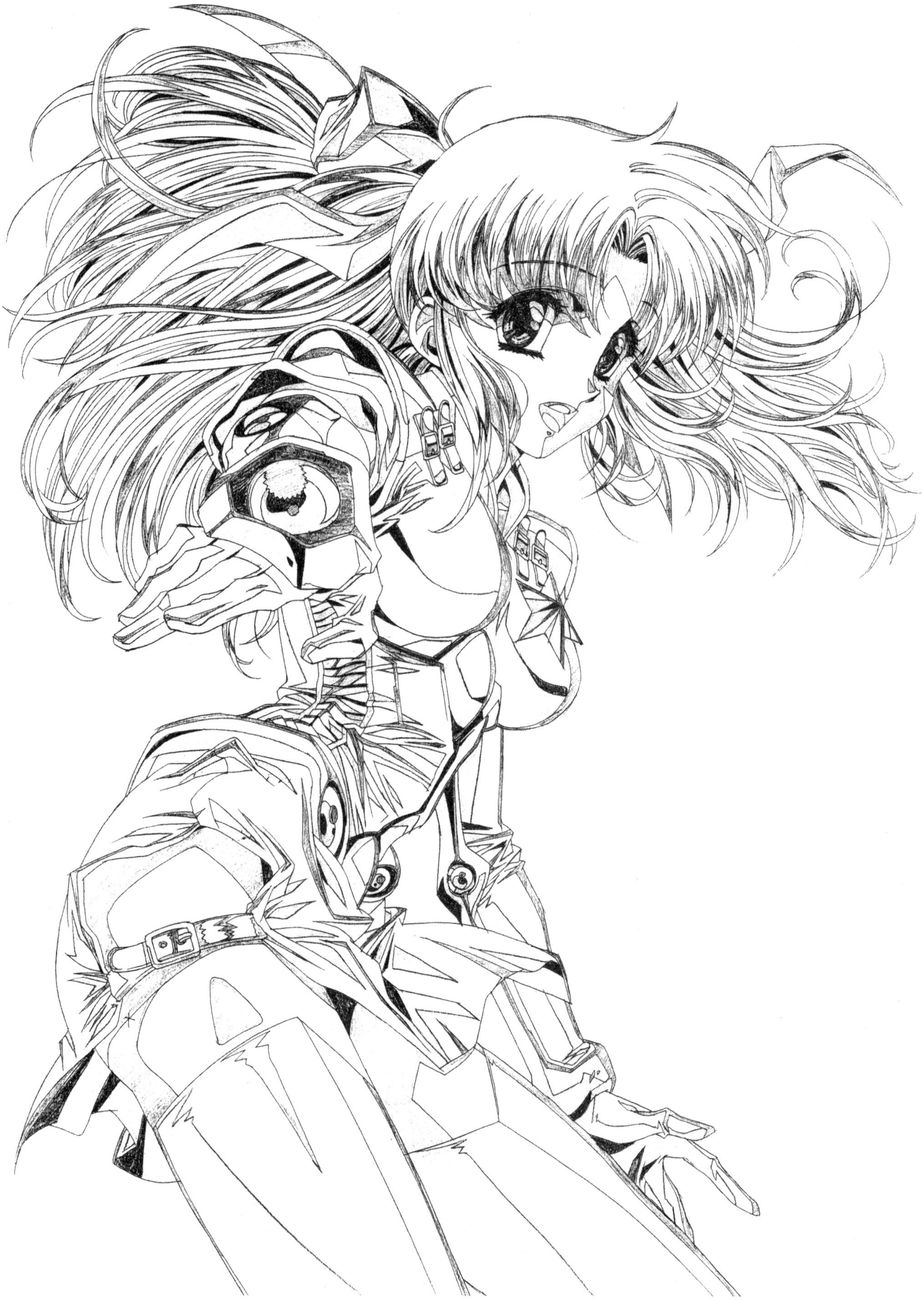

This is a composition for a cover illustration I just completed. I wanted to achieve something evoking the sense of "white," so I adjusted the hue for the ground in hopes of achieving a risp, fresh look. Unfortunately, the effect I added to the original drawing will not show up on the actual print version.

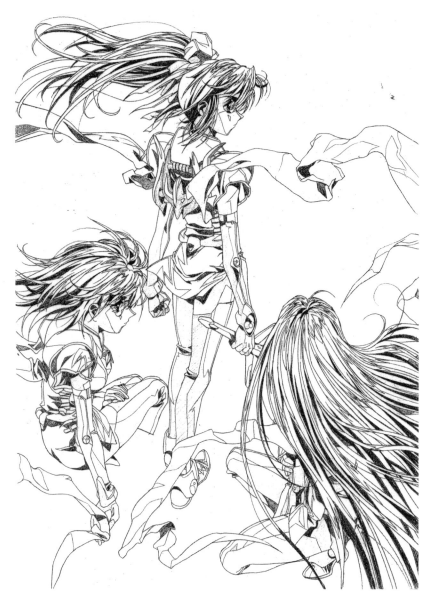

◀ Other than the cover illustration shown on the previous page, all of the compositions in black and white on these pages are part of an early series I produced. These works were originally rendered as individual cells (i.e. celluloid artwork), but I recreated them using digital paint.

キャラ位置（セル位置）
変更の可能性あります..
早朝
空気のつめたい
澄んだ感じ

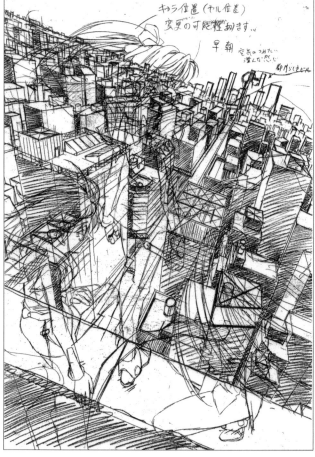

This background draft that you see is normally something produced solely to establish the perspective so that the creator (myself) can then determine where to position the characters. The background drawing to the right is a collaborative work done with an artist who is in charge of producing the background artwork. ▶

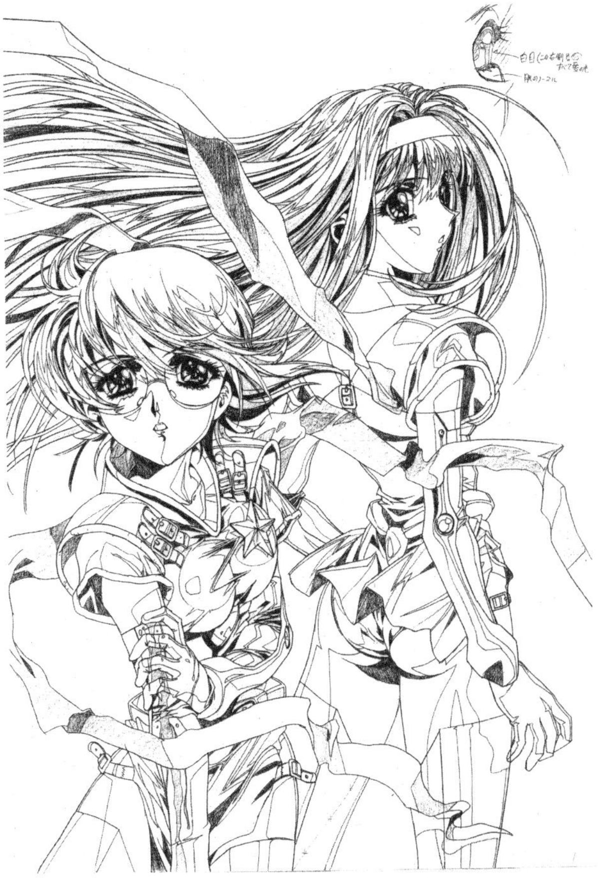

All of the illustrations had been in color when they were produced as cells. Regardless of how much software gains popularity and progress is made, the key to a high-quality close-up still hinges on the artist's sensibilities.

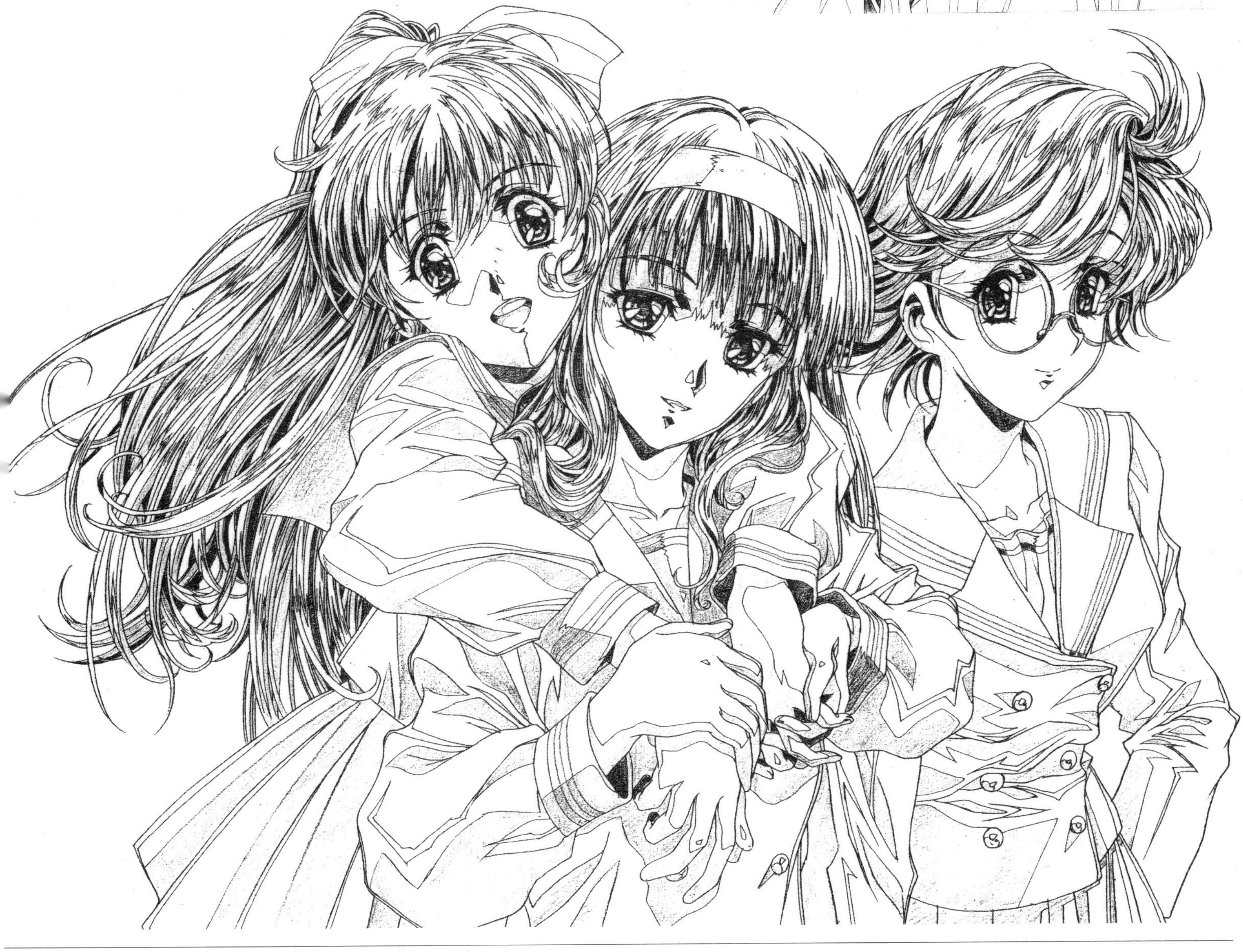

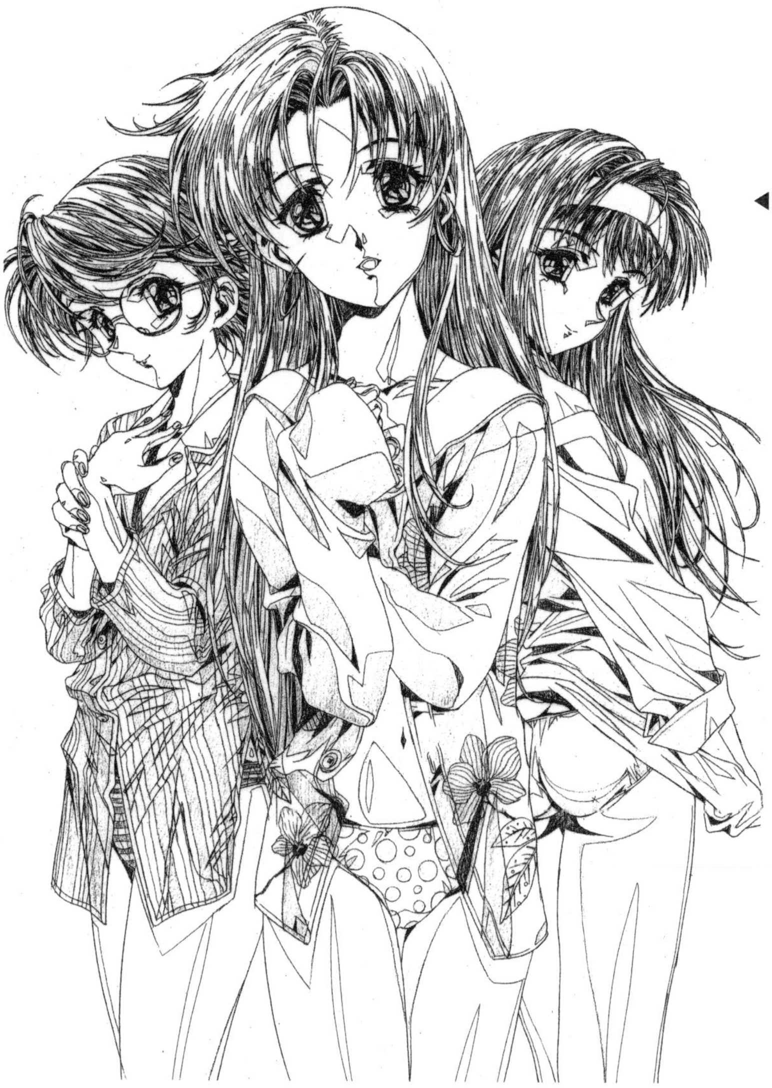

◀ Even though it was rendered digitally, considerable work went into the pajamas' and undergarment's print and patterning in this illustration. I made an effort to reproduce the original celluloid composition as faithfully as possible.

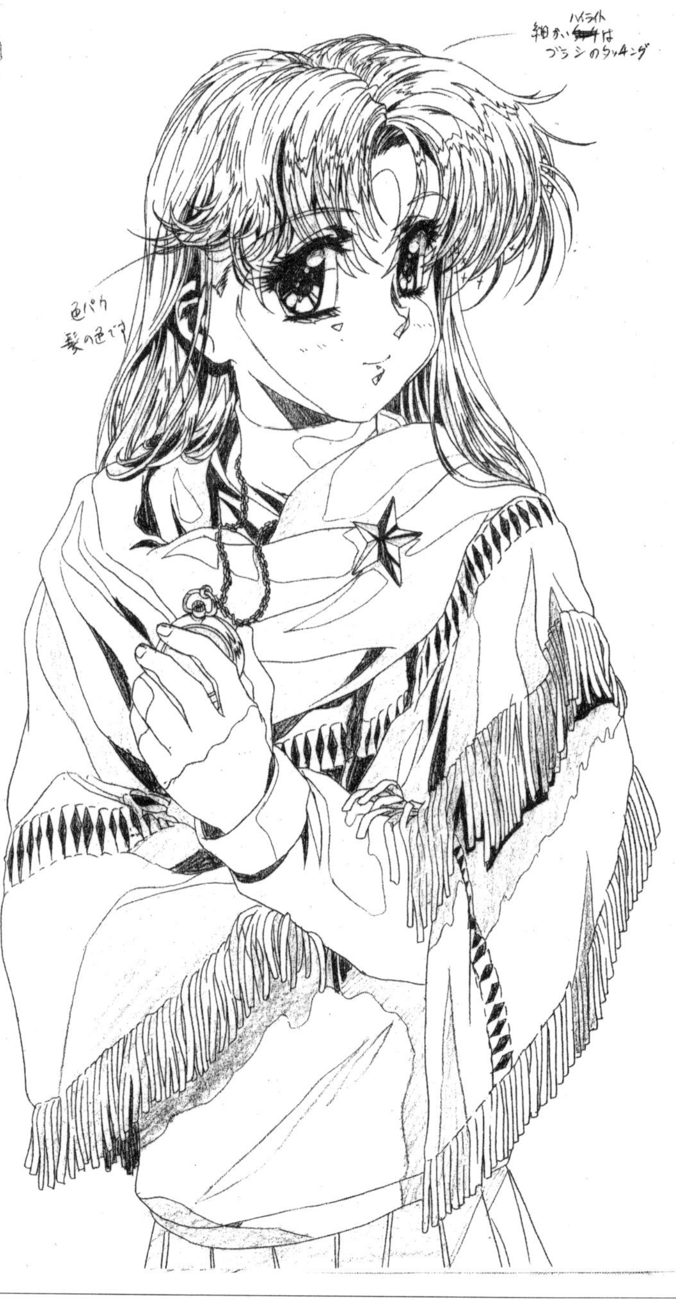
ハイライト
細かい は
色パク
髪の色です

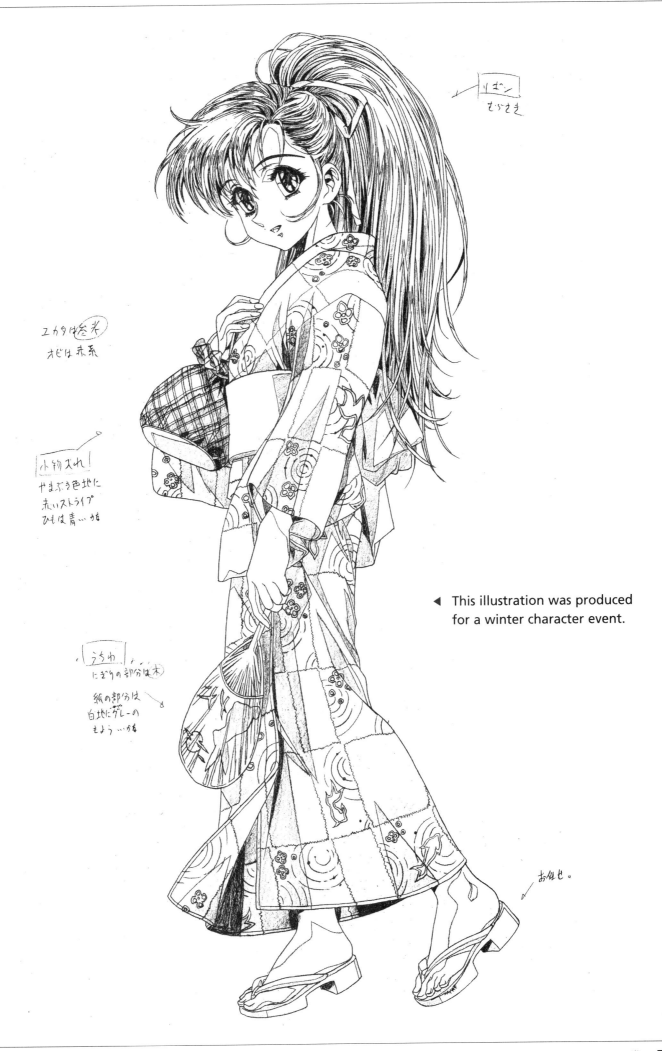

リボン
むらさき

ユカタは参考
オビは朱系

小物入れ
やまぶき色地に
朱いストライプ
ひもは青い焼

うちわ
にぎりの部分は木

紙の部分は
白地にグレーの
もよういろ

お任せ。

◄ This illustration was produced
for a winter character event.

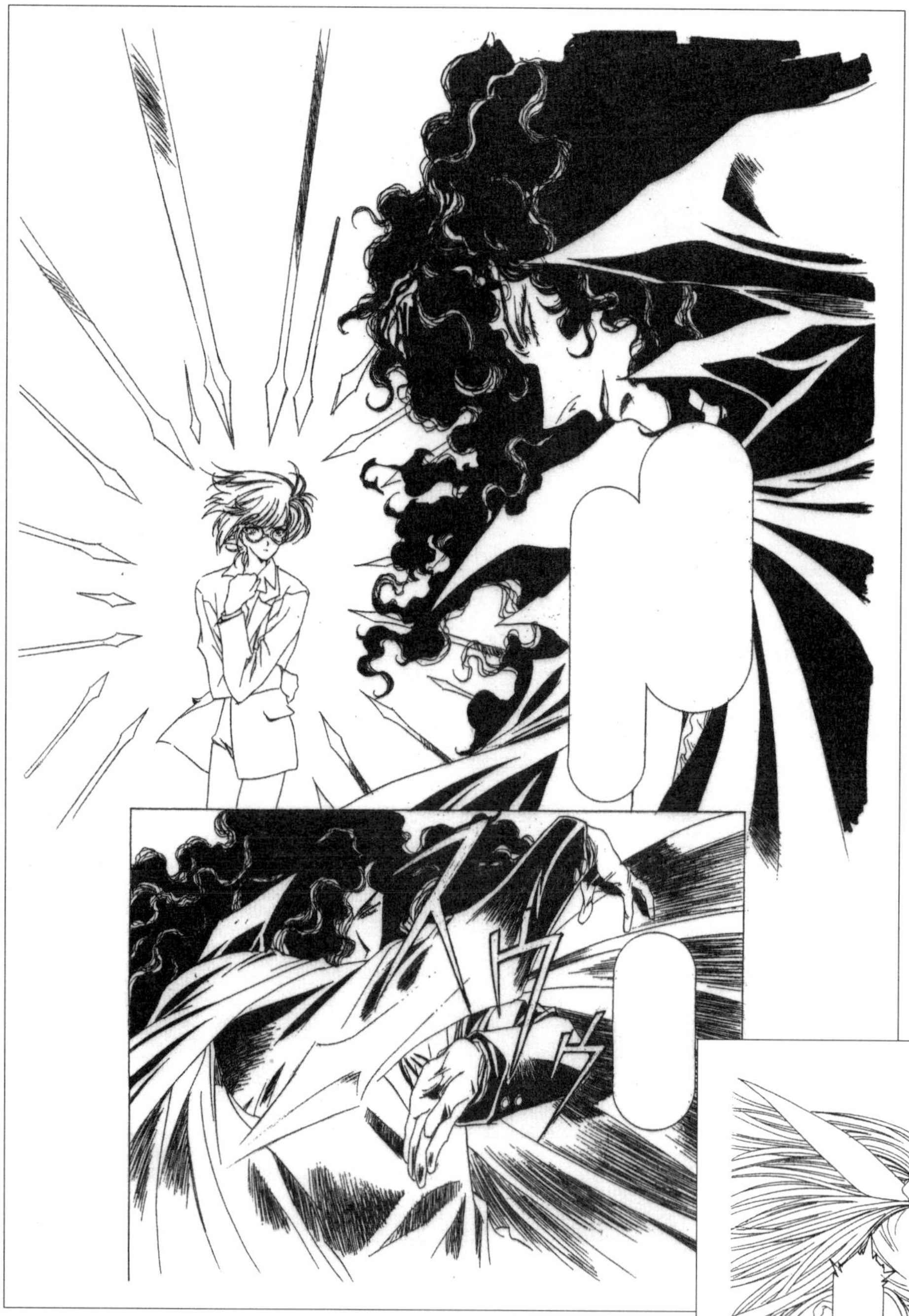

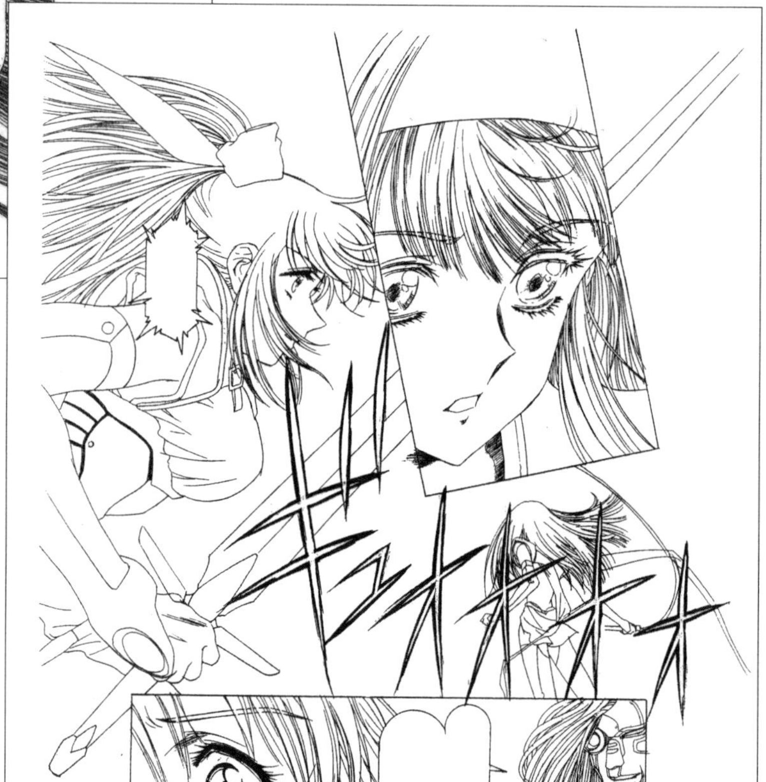

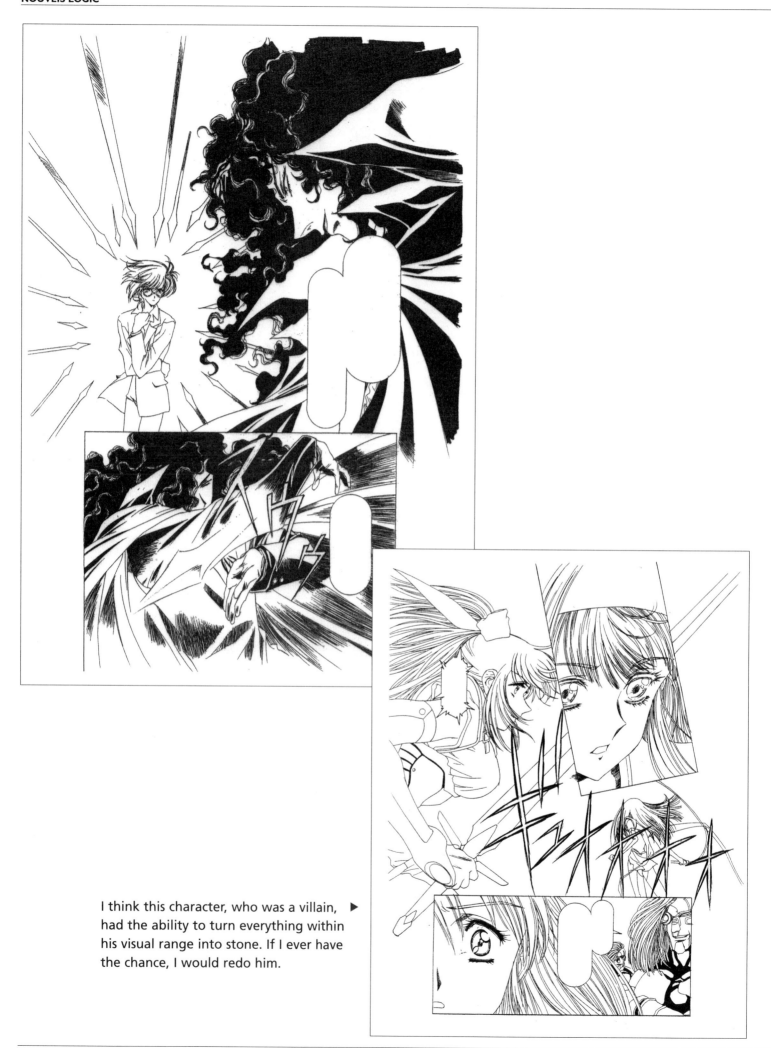

I think this character, who was a villain, ▶ had the ability to turn everything within his visual range into stone. If I ever have the chance, I would redo him.

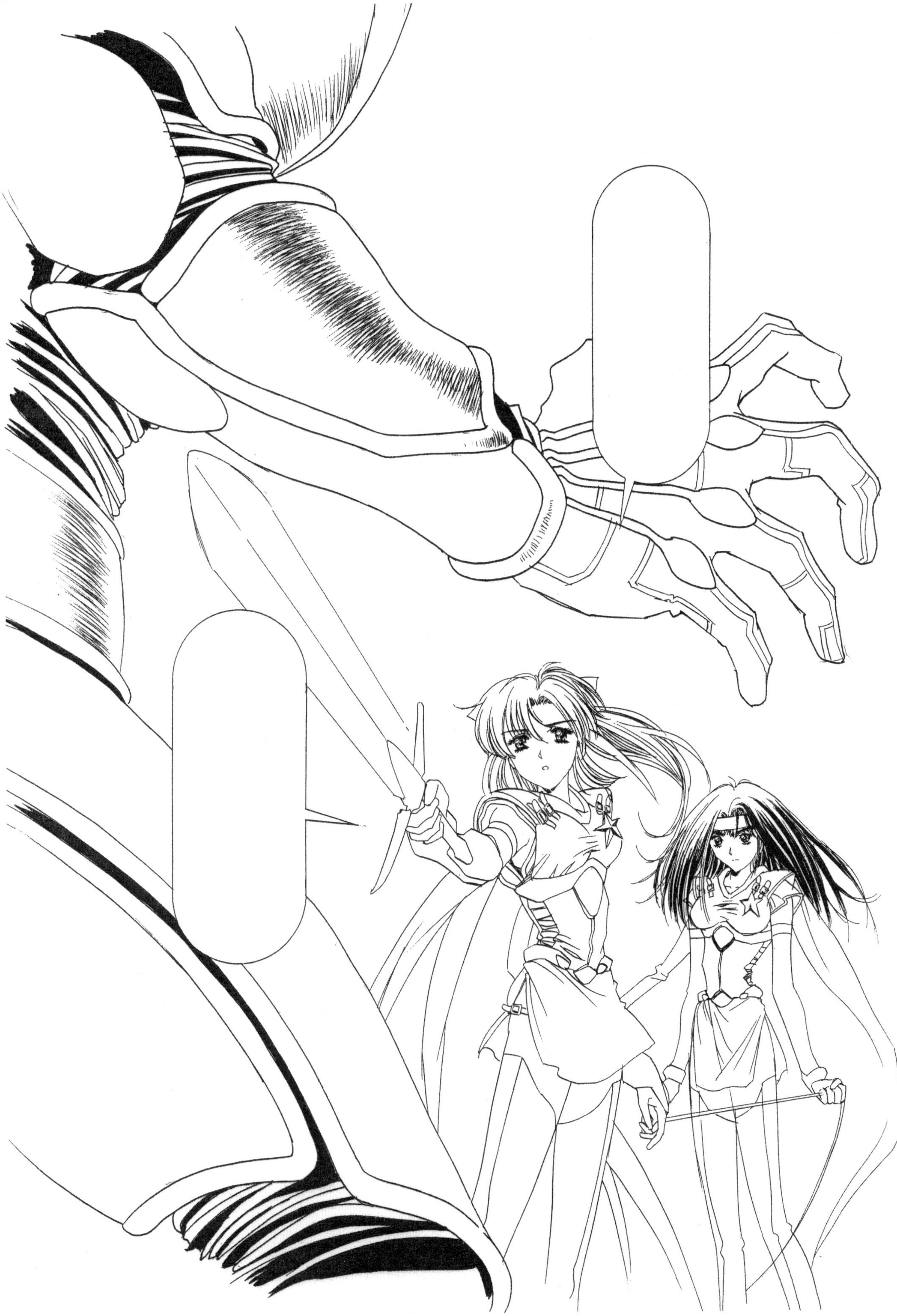

At the time this composition was originally created, oil-based markers were used to color the original artwork, which made some effects impossible to produce, so I relied on tone to create these effects.

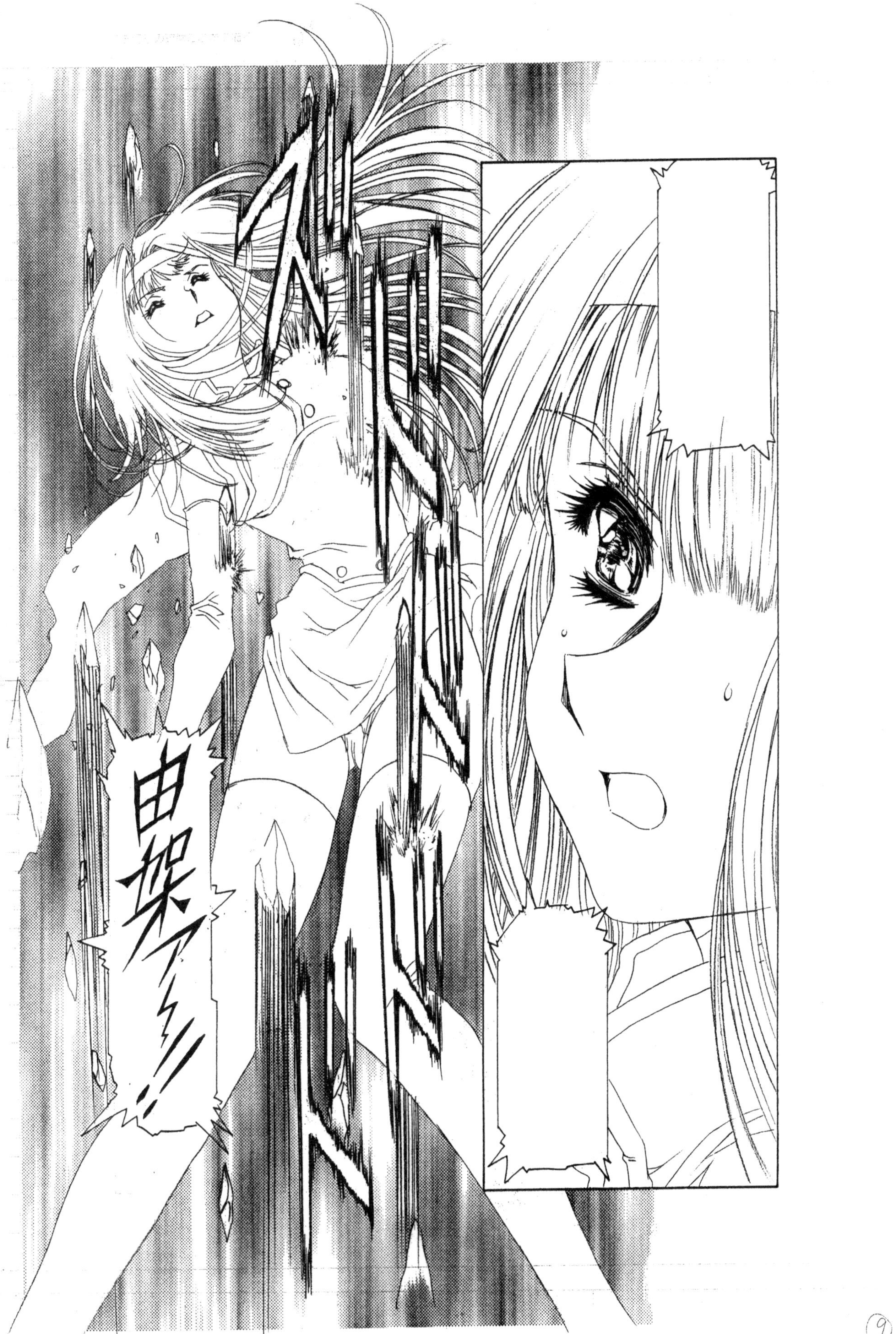
由架ァ〜!!

Incidentally, a fan once mentioned counting the number of times the female characters' panties could be seen in *Nouveis Logic*'s dramatic scenes. I wonder if that fan is still reading *Nouveis Logic*.

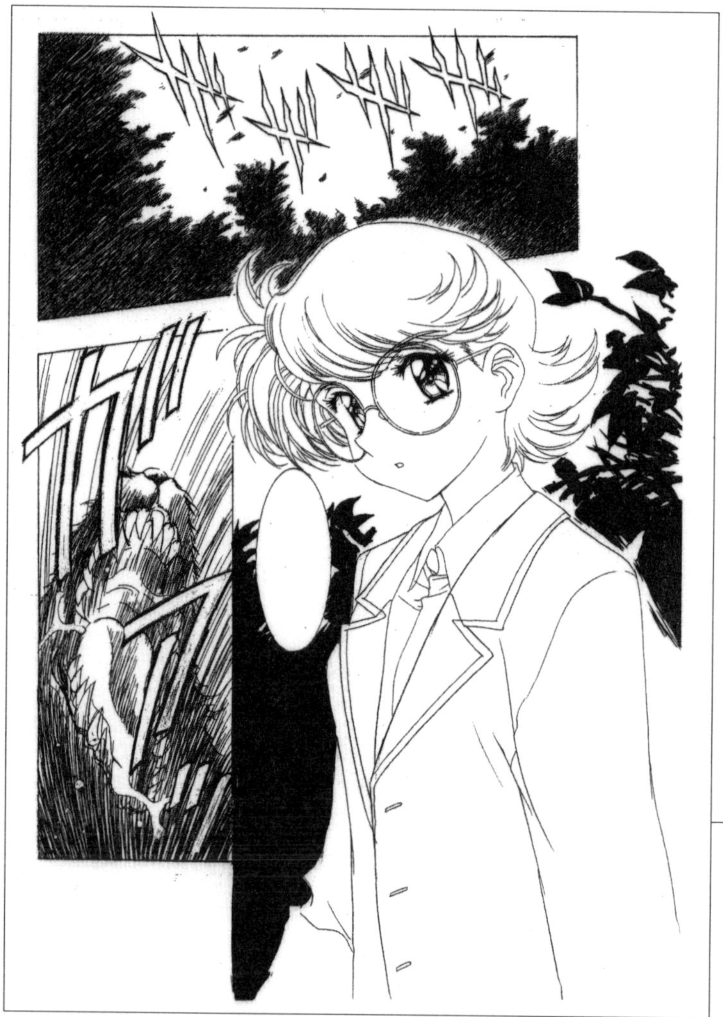

◀ Ah! I just remembered! Around this time, I had been producing some of my work in pencil. My schedule was pretty tight, so I omitted inking the drawing and instead would photocopy it and then add color. I was very much walking on thin ice following that process (wry laugh).

All of the characters appearing in both the top panel and the panel to the right were rendered in pencil. The only areas where I used ink were the eyes. ▶

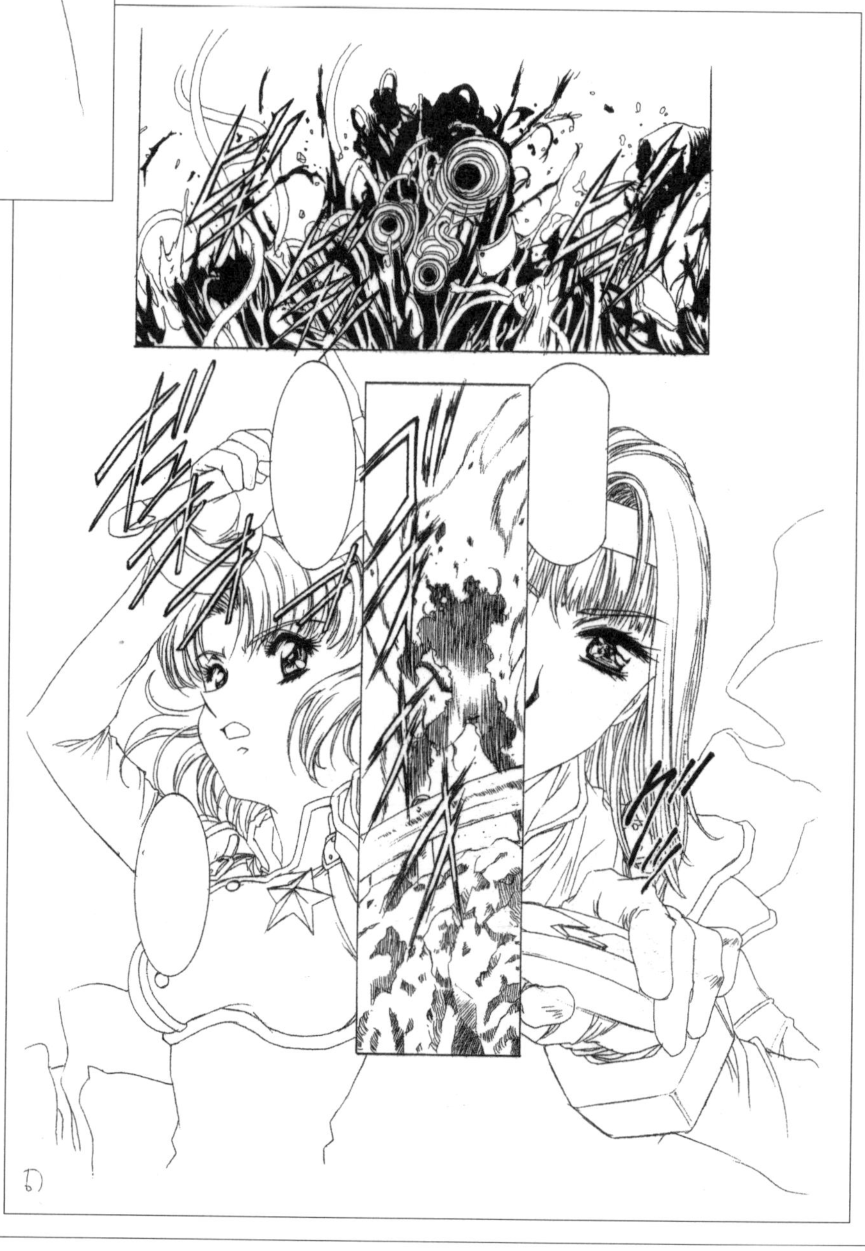

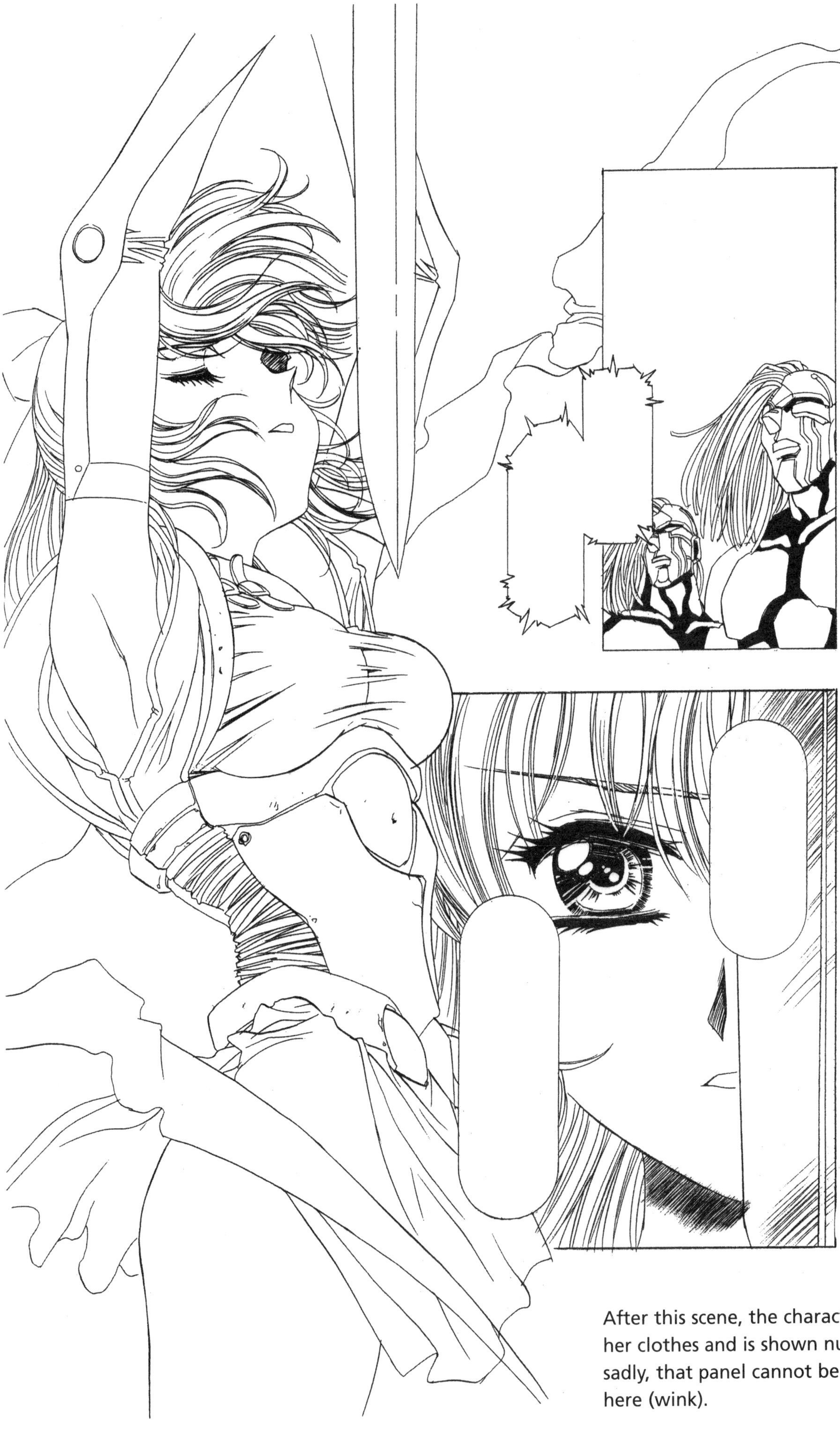

After this scene, the character tears off her clothes and is shown nude. But sadly, that panel cannot be reproduced here (wink).

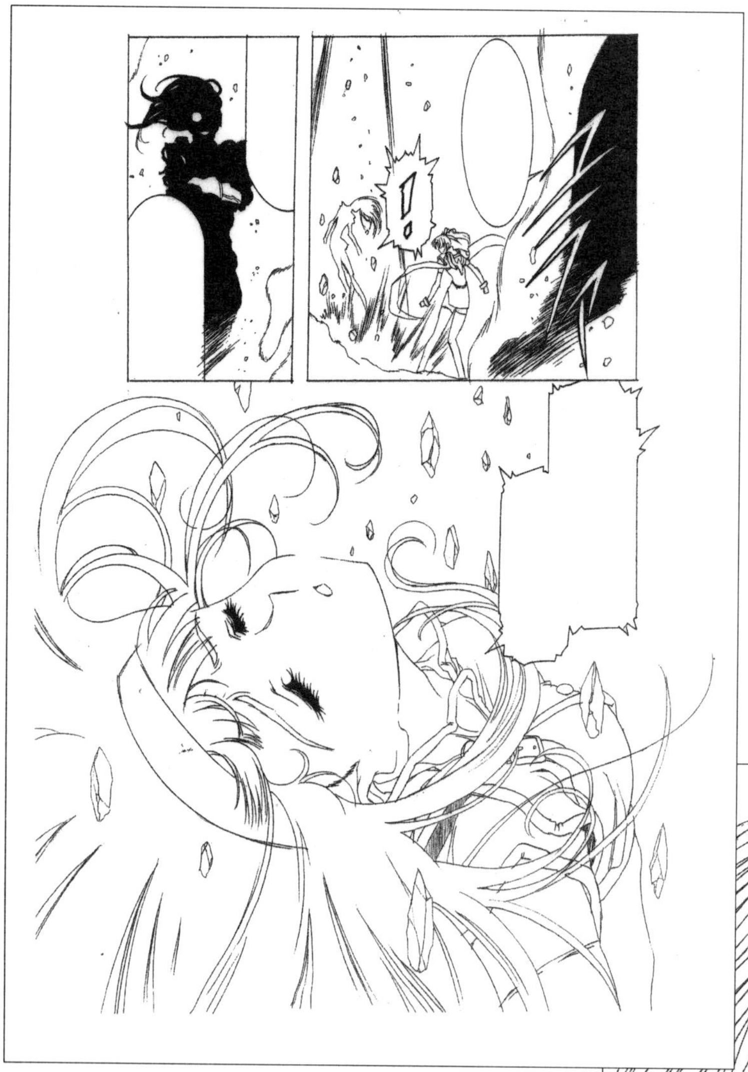

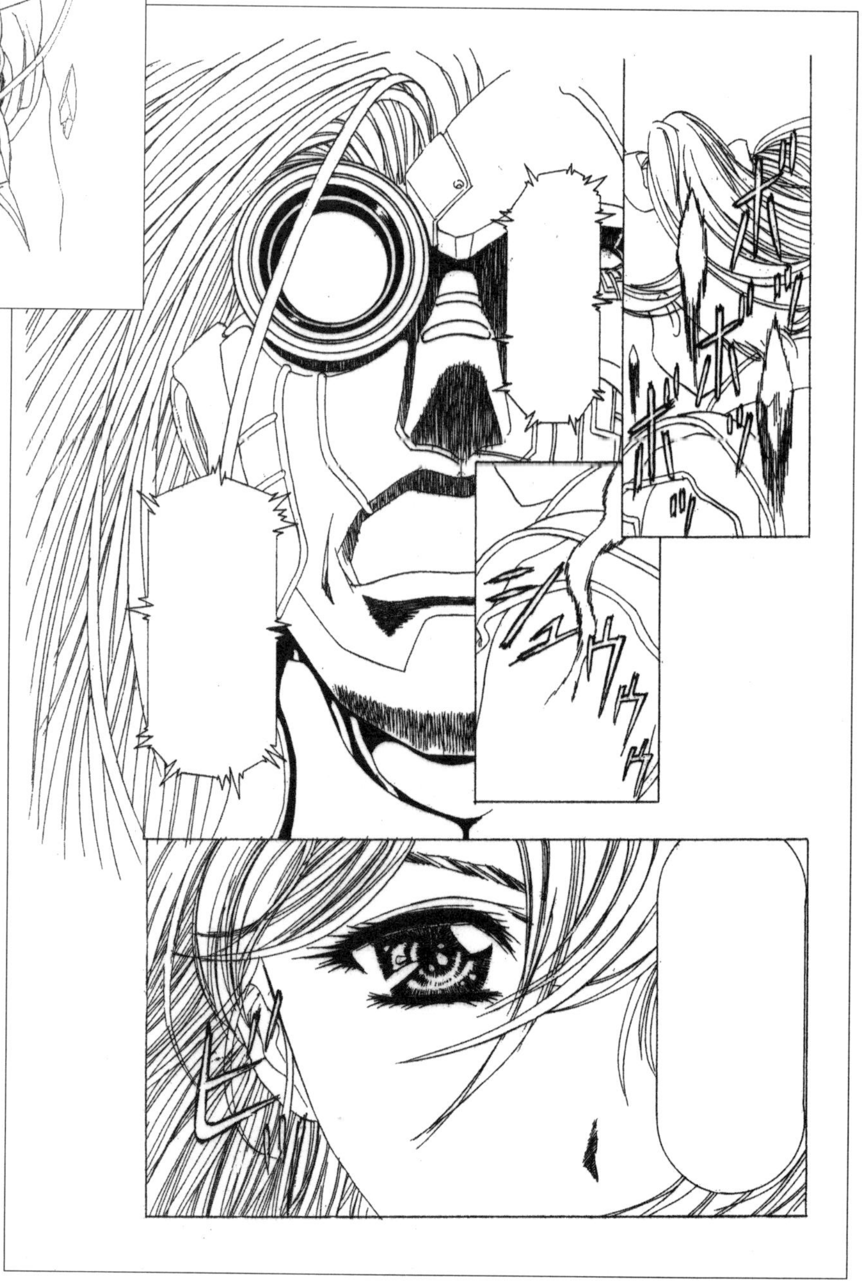

Nouveis Logic is one of the series I would like to continue. I am striving to make both the artwork and the story after the initial series more sophisticated series for its future release. Keep a lookout for it on your bookstore shelves!